Byways in Hand-weaving

Frontispiece
Guatemalan Fiesta headband (*See Part VII*)

Byways in Hand-weaving

MARY MEIGS ATWATER

Macmillan Publishing Co., Inc.

NEW YORK

SEVENTH PRINTING 1976

Macmillan Publishing Co., Inc.
866 Third Avenue, New York, N.Y. 10022

PRINTED IN THE UNITED STATES OF AMERICA

—————————— *Foreword* ——————————

According to Webster (unabridged) a "byway" is: "A way or road off the main highway; a side road; an obscure or unfrequented road." There is about the word a connotation of leisurely adventure, undertaken for pleasure, and in the hope of coming upon hitherto unknown beauties or experiences.

The textile techniques described in the following pages offer the hand weaver a variety of such side trips and adventures that have brought the author of these notes much pleasure and are here set forth in the hope of bringing enjoyment to like-minded craftsmen.

Though differing widely in type and purpose, these several techniques have certain things in common: all are extremely ancient, leading back beyond the dawn of history; few have been adequately described elsewhere; none require large or elaborate equipment—some, in fact, require no equipment at all except the eyes and hands with which a generous Nature has provided most of us. Moreover all are practical and may be used for the production of handsome and useful articles. This last seems to me an essential quality for true enjoyment. It may be amusing to make mud pies or to build sand castles, but, unless the thing one makes has a measure of permanence and usefulness, the making is a mere pastime and cannot give any very adequate satisfaction.

This collection of what may be called the minor textile crafts makes no pretense of completeness. Some useful and interesting crafts—macramé, for instance—have been omitted because they are amply documented and anyone desiring information on the subject may find it elsewhere without difficulty. Others have been omitted for purely personal reasons. For instance, I do not like bead-weaving. It seems to me a fussy business

v

and hard on the eyes; also the results tend to be peculiarly hideous. In card-weaving or inkle-weaving it is difficult to produce anything distressingly ugly, but in bead-weaving it is unusual to produce anything else. At least in my experience.

"Colonial mats" and rake-knitting have been omitted because they require enormous quantities of costly material without an adequate return. The products are usable, to be sure, though distressingly unbeautiful as a rule, and the making is so simple and rapid that these crafts do not present a challenge, or give the sense of achievement that is so important a part of the satisfaction of handicraft.

Several of the crafts presented here are widely used in the practice of occupational therapy, and some of the less familiar techniques might also be found valuable for this purpose. And though one may think of occupational therapy as a business for experts and for hospital practice, a little simple o. t. is often helpful in everyday homemaking—to interest a sick child, for instance, or to occupy an oldster who needs something new and creative to help the time go by. Or it may be for oneself, to ease periods of anxiety, or of waiting, or of dull conversation. Most of these crafts are noiseless, take little space, do not create a litter, for the most part go along pleasantly and rapidly, and require enough skill to be interesting.

Some of these crafts have been used—and are being used—for the production of articles for sale, but some of them are not well adapted to purposes of profit in cash, due to the time involved. However, as in most handicraft, the chief profit is in the pleasure of the craftsman.

Mary Meigs Atwater

Salt Lake City, Utah

Contents

List of Illustrations

List of Diagrams

PART I

Card-weaving

HISTORY. Card-weaving or "tablet weaving" as it is sometimes called, is a very ancient textile technique and of surprisingly wide distribution. It was practiced in prehistoric times in countries as far apart as Egypt and Iceland, Sweden and China, Arabia and the Middle East. In some of these countries it is still current but—oddly enough—it is one of the few textile techniques that appears never to have found its way into mechanical commercial weaving. Also—and also oddly enough—it seems never to have been practiced in the Americas, either North or South, till the present.

TYPE OF FABRIC. Card-weaving is limited to the production of narrow fabrics, but for such fabrics there are many practical uses—as belts, hatbands, wristbands for watches, sandal-straps, bag-handles, guimpe for the finishing of upholstery or for the binding of loom-woven pieces, pack-straps, bridles and similar uses. For some of these things there is no other form of weaving that is as good, for the four-ply fabric produced is extremely strong in the lengthwise direction, because of the unique construction. In a card-woven fabric four threads in each set—or three or six threads according to the number of holes in the cards used—are twisted together for the entire length of the piece.

This twisted structure, to be sure, is not found in the Icelandic double-weave technique, which is, structurally, a double warp-faced rep. But with this exception it is the characteristic structure of all card-woven fabrics.

EQUIPMENT. The equipment for card-weaving is extremely simple and inexpensive, consisting as it does of a set of square cards—or of triangu-

1

lar or hexagonal cards if one likes—with holes in the corners. Such a set of cards constitutes a very ingenious and eminently practical shedding mechanism and permits the production of interesting and handsome pattern effects in practically unlimited variety.

A small belt-shuttle of the type shown on **Diagram No. 1** at (*b*) is a convenience, though any small shuttle may be used. The weft yarn may even be put through the shed without a shuttle. But the knife-edged belt-shuttle is very useful in driving the weft firmly together.

A frame of some kind may be used to support the cards if desired. The little "inkle" loom described in Part II may be used for the purpose —with the heddle pegs taken out, of course. However a frame of any kind somewhat restricts the weaving. Simple patterns woven with four turns each way can be managed over a frame, but for the more elaborate kinds of card-weaving the stretch of warp is insufficient. I prefer simply to attach one end of the warp to a support of some kind—a hook in the wall, a door-knob, a porch pillar or a convenient tree if working out-of-doors—with the other end attached to the chair on which I sit. It is then possible to control the tension of the warp simply by moving the chair. If the warp is set up between two fixed supports as in a frame it is necessary to release the tension frequently. As this is a warp-faced fabric all the take-up is in the warp, and when the warp is stretched too tight it is impossible to beat the weft back correctly.

The square card shown at (*a*) on the diagram is the kind and size most frequently used. If smaller cards are used it will be found that the hands do not hold them easily, and if the holes in the cards are too close to the edges the warp will tend to hook over the corners of the cards and much trouble will follow.

Triangular cards are sometimes used, but there seems little or no advantage and they are more difficult to handle than the square cards. Hexagonal cards carrying six threads are also sometimes used. These are more difficult to handle than the square cards, but somewhat more elaborate patterns based on six colors may be produced, and the fabric is of course heavier, being six-ply instead of four-ply.

MATERIALS. The materials used in card-weaving should be strong, firm yarns of medium weight, but not fuzzy, stiff or wiry materials. The mercerized cottons are the most popular materials, though some silks

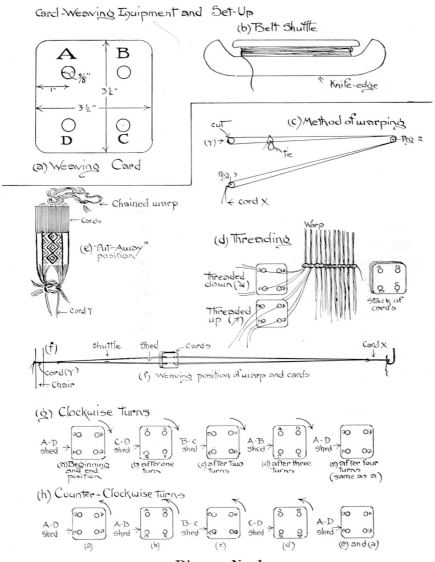

Card-Weaving Equipment and Set-Up

(a) Weaving Card

(b) Belt Shuffle — Knife-edge

(c) Method of warping — cut, (Y), tie, Peg 2, Peg 3, cord X

Chained warp — Cards

(e) "Put-Away" position — cord Y

(d) Threading — Warp, Threaded down (↘), Threaded up (↗), Stack of cards

(f) shuttle, Shed, Cards, Cord X, cord (Y), Chair — (f) Weaving position of warp and cards

(g) Clockwise Turns — A-D shed, (a) Beginning and end position; C-D shed, (b) after one turn; B-c shed, (c) after Two turns; A-B shed, (d) after three turns; A-D shed, (e) after four turns (same as a)

(h) Counter-Clockwise Turns — A-D shed (a), A-B shed (b), B-c shed (c), C-D shed (d), A-D shed (e) and (a)

Diagram No. 1

and rayons are suitable and very hard twisted wool yarns may even be used. Extremely fine materials are difficult to handle as so many cards are required, and very coarse materials do not pack together properly. Linens and the hard-twisted crochet cottons do not give good results.

For very narrow bands such as wristwatch bands, a #20 mercerized cotton may be used, but for most purposes a #10 perle cotton is the most satisfactory material. A #5 perle cotton may also be used, but for most things a #3 perle cotton is too coarse.

The width of a piece of card-weaving depends on the weight of the material and on the number of cards. Also, to a lesser degree, on the technique of the weaver. The warp, however, must always be drawn close enough together to cover the weft completely. A band made on 40 cards —160 ends of #10 perle cotton—will, when correctly woven, be about 1½″ wide.

TYPES OF WEAVING. The simplest weave, common to most countries and based on a regular number of turns of the cards, is the weave ordinarily used, and when the set-up is in bright colors and a good pattern, this weave gives excellent results.

The Icelandic double weave, referred to above, produces a fabric of different structure from the other forms of card-weaving and patterns of a different type. The Arabian double-faced weave gives patterns similar to those in double weaving—usually carried out in two colors, with the same pattern on both sides of the piece but with the colors reversed.

There is also an Egyptian technique that results in some very interesting pattern effects, achieved by turning some of the cards clockwise and some counter-clockwise. This is, perhaps, the most interesting of the card-weaving techniques.

THE SET–UP. The warp for a piece of card-weaving may be made in several different ways. The easiest way is to measure off the number of threads of each color required for the pattern in hand, thread the cards, stretch the warp between supports and comb out the resulting tangle by pushing the cards along the warp from one end to the other. However, if a large number of threads are involved, this is a troublesome process.

In my opinion the best way to make the warp is to make it over the

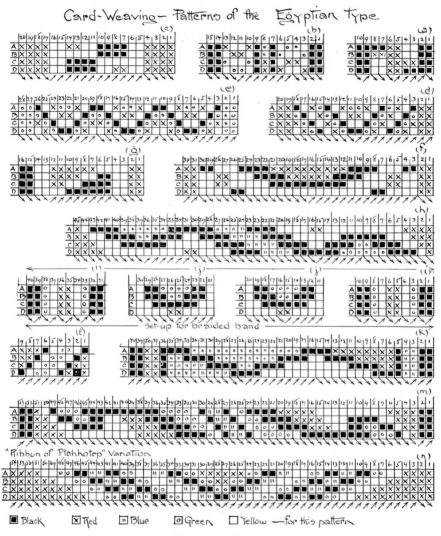

Diagram No. 2

bars of a warping board and to measure off separately the four threads for each card, making a chain-tie around each group of four threads. This makes threading the cards a very simple matter and it is unnecessary to do any combing-out of the warp.

To make a warp, for instance, for pattern (*a*), **Diagram No. 2,** beginning at the left—as is more convenient than beginning at the right—count off four threads in black (or in the darkest color to be used) for card No. 10, and make a loop tie around these threads. Warp four more threads in the same color for card No. 9 and make the tie. For cards 8 and 7 warp for each one thread red (or the brightest color), one thread darkest and two threads in the lightest color. For cards 6 and 5 warp four threads red (or the brightest color) for each. And so on through the draft, making a loop tie over each group of four threads. All warping should be done in this manner, except warps for some of the special techniques as shown on **Diagram No. 4,** which will be explained later.

When the warp is complete, tie a cord through the loop around the last peg of the warping frame and chain the warp up to the ties. Cut the ends at the first peg.

To thread the cards proceed as follows: count off the number of cards required for the pattern and number them in pencil—for pattern (*a*) from 1 to 10—and stack them up in order, with the card numbered 10 on top. (Use a pencil for the numbering as the cards will be used over for other pieces and the numbering may be different.) Lay the chained warp before you on a table with the cut ends toward you. Lay the stack of cards on the right-hand side of the warp. Pick up card No. 10 and thread the first group of four threads—the first group on the left-hand side of the warp. Observe the small arrows along the lower margin of the draft. These indicate the direction in which the threads should be taken through the cards. All threads in the same card should be threaded in the same direction through the card—either "down" ⬊—from front to back, or "up" ⬈ from back to front—as shown at (*d*), **Diagram No. 1.**

When the threading is complete, attach the end of the warp by the cord (X), tied through the loops of the warp, to some firm support and stretch the warp. Draw the cut ends through the fingers to draw down any slackness. Slide the cards back and forth a foot or so along to the warp if necessary to straighten the threads. Tie the cut ends together and tie a cord (Y) through the knot. This cord may then be tied to a

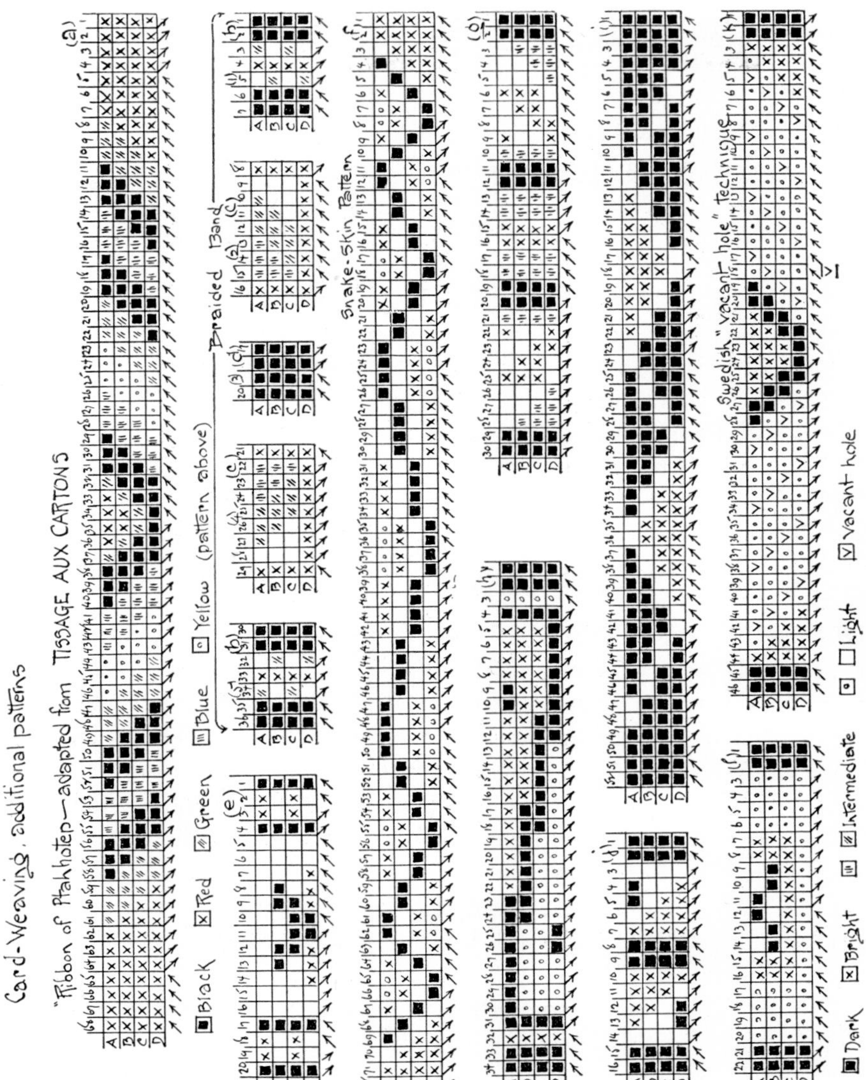

Card-weaving, additional patterns

"Ribbon of Ptahhotep—adapted from TISSAGE AUX CARTONS

Snake-skin Pattern

Braided Band

Yellow (pattern above)

Swedish "vacant hole" technique

■ Black   ⊠ Red   ▦ Green   □ Blue

■ Dark   ⊠ Bright   ▦ Intermediate   ⊡ □ Light   ☑ Vacant hole

Diagram No. 3

support—the back of the weaver's chair by preference, as noted above. This completes the set-up and weaving may begin.

The set-up process may sound complicated, because it has been written out in detail to avoid any possible confusion. In practice it is simple enough and may be accomplished rapidly and easily if each step is taken correctly.

Warps for card-weaving are usually made long enough for one or two pieces only. In calculating the necessary length, allow four or five inches for the knot at (Y), which may later be braided for fringes; also allow twelve inches or so for the unweavable end of the warp. An allowance must also be made for take-up, and should be generous as this is a warp-faced fabric. It is impossible to say just what this allowance should be as it varies with the material used and the closeness of the beat.

If a very long warp is desired, and space is lacking to stretch it full length, chain the "X" end of the warp as far as desired and tie the cord through the last loop of the chain. When this point is reached in weaving, the loop may be taken out and an additional length of warp released.

COLOR IN CARD–WEAVING.   Any desired colors may, of course, be used in card-weaving. However, dull shades or light "pastel" shades are apt to give disappointing results. Combinations of brilliant colors are best. Black should usually be included, with a brilliant red, a strong "royal" blue, a sharp blue-green and a golden yellow by preference. White, too, for a light effect. Brown, tan and purple seem to be contraindicated.

The patterns depend entirely on changes of color. The changes of color are indicated on the drafts by the hatchings—the darkest color by the plain black squares, the lightest color by the plain white squares, the most brilliant color—usually red—by "X" and the other shades by the other hatchings used.

To judge the effect of a particular pattern and color arrangement before setting it up and weaving it, draw the draft on 4 by 4 squared paper, in colored crayons. Take two strips of mirror, cut with square edges, and set these strips upright along the top and bottom margins of the draft. As even small mirrors usually have beveled edges, it is well to have a mirror cut in two lengthwise for this purpose. Then by peering into either of the strips of mirror one may see the pattern as it will appear when woven.

Small Motifs, for use as Borders, and as combined for Wide Pieces.

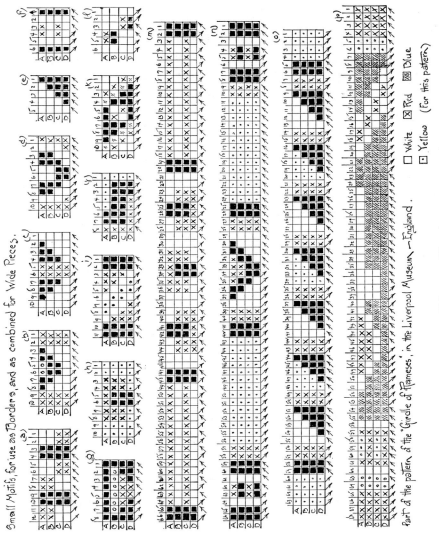

Part of the pattern of the "Girdle of Rameses", in the Liverpool Museum—England.

☐ White   ☒ Red   ▨ Blue
⊡ Yellow   (For this pattern)

Diagram No. 4

WEAVING. All the patterns for simple weaving on square cards, as given on **Diagrams 2, 3** and **4** may be woven in the following manner:

Stretch the warp as shown at (f) on **Diagram No. 1** with the cards facing to the right and the A–D shed on top. Sit to the right of the warp. Take the shuttle through the shed made by the cards. The first few shots of weft may be in a coarse material to provide something to beat against. To change the shed for the second shot of weft give the cards a quarter-turn forward, or clockwise, and bring the shuttle back through the new shed. Make three more quarter-turns in the same direction, weaving a shot of weft each time, and pressing the weft together as closely as possible with the edge of the shuttle. After the fourth turn the cards will be back in the A–D position. After weaving this shed, give the cards a quarter-turn in reverse, or counter-clockwise. It will be noted that the top of the shed remains the same. Weave three more quarter-turns in reverse and the cards will be back in the D–A position. Continue in this manner as desired.

As this is a warp-faced fabric there is no take-up in the weft, which should not be woven slack as in most weaving on a harness-loom. The width of the band is controlled by the tension of the weft, which should be drawn tight enough to bring the warp close together above the weft and to keep a good edge. To make certain of keeping a correct width and a good edge, weavers sometimes leave a loop of weft at the edge, and after making a new shed and beating the twist back closely for the next weft shot, then draw out the loop.

There is a trick about turning the cards. Do not press the cards close together but permit them to hang free in the warp. Hold the pack of cards between the two hands with the thumbs on top and the fingers below, and make the turn with a shuffling motion. If, after the turn, the shed is not clear, slide the cards up and down the warp for a few inches.

When stopping work, bring the cards down against the edge of the weaving and chain the unwoven warp, making the first loop as close as possible against the cards. This prevents confusion, and is illustrated at (e) on **Diagram No. 1.**

If through some mischance the cords break or the set-up becomes disarranged, it is possible to set things straight again by means of the numbers and letters on the cards, but as this is sometimes troublesome it is better to avoid such accidents. Also it is desirable to make a habit of

Three-Hole and Six-Hole Cards — also
Cards with a hole at the center.

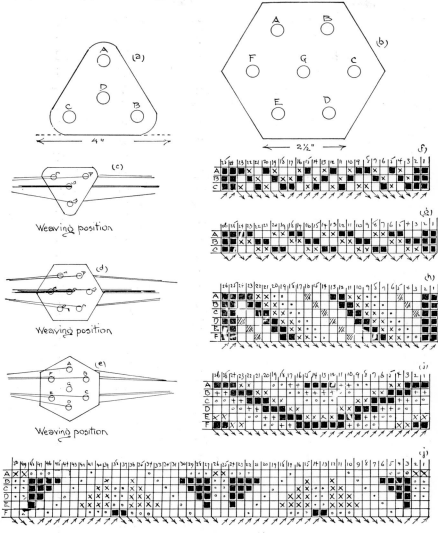

Diagram No. 5

leaving the work at the end of a series of turns so that there will not be confusion in starting again where one left off.

VARIATIONS.   A simple card-weaving set-up may be woven in a variety of ways as well as in the normal manner described above. For instance the cards may be turned in the same direction throughout. However, when this is done the threads will soon become twisted and it will be necessary to take out the tie at X and untwist them. The system of four turns each way will give four different patterns, depending on which shed is used as the "return" shed. Lengthwise stripes may be woven by making two turns forward and two turns in reverse. Four different stripes will result by using one or another of the four sheds as the starting shed. Moreover the cards may be turned with eight turns forward and eight back, or twelve turns each way, and so on. Or the cards may be re-arranged in the warp. In such patterns as (*d*) and (*e*), **Diagram No. 2**, for instance, if the cards are re-arranged so that all the threads of the darkest color come on the same shed, horizontal stripes will result.

To consider some of the patterns in detail: draft (*a*), **Diagram No. 2**, makes a very narrow band and is best used as a border pattern for a wide piece or in an arrangement for a braided band such as the (*i*)–(*j*) set-up. The same is true of drafts (*b*), (*g*) and (*l*). Drafts (*d*) and (*e*) are typical Egyptian arrangements and weave diamond figures. As does also draft (*n*). Drafts (*h*) and (*m*) are constructed on the "Egyptian river" motif, and are handsomest when woven in the normal manner of four turns each way. Draft (*k*), which I call the "Harlequin" pattern, produces large diamonds when woven normally and is very effective.

For the braided effect any two small drafts may be used, set up as for four bands. They may be woven all together in one pack for several inches. Then woven separately as four bands for three inches or so and the bands braided together. After which they are put together again in a single pack and woven as one. Such a band is shown on **Illustrations 1** and **5**. Draft (*f*), **Diagram No. 2**, produces a medallion figure and is a Central European pattern.

Of the pattern on **Diagram No. 3**, (*a*) makes a very handsome band when woven in the normal manner. It is adapted from "Le Tissage aux Cartons" and is taken from an ancient Egyptian wall-painting, in the colors indicated.

Illustration No. 1

Simple card-weaving (for drafts refer to diagrams). Left to right: draft (*e*) Diagram 2, variations; draft (*k*) Diagram 2, variations; braided belt; braided belt, draft (*i–j*) Diagram 2; upper, Egyptian River motif; lower, double and double-faced weave; Egyptian two-color weave

13

The (b)–(c)–(d) series is for the braided band shown on **Illustration No. 1.** Draft (f) was designed for one of my army hospital patients who wished to "weave a rattle-snake." Draft (g) is a very ancient Scandinavian pattern and draft (h) a modernistic effect in large triangles. Draft (i) is a very ancient Germanic pattern. Draft (k), in which the cards—except the borders and the center diamond—are threaded with only three threads, when done in coarse material, produces an interesting variation of texture.

The small patterns (a), (e) on **Diagram No. 4** are intended for use as borders or in various arrangements for braided pieces, or combined with plain-colored sections, or repeated a number of times as shown at (m), (n) and (o).

Draft (p) is part of the pattern of an interesting piece known as the "Girdle of Rameses" in the Liverpool Museum. It was at one time supposed to be an ancient piece of card-weaving, but was probably done on a different type of primitive loom. However, the odd key-shaped figure is interesting and can be produced easily on the cards.

Diagram No. 5 shows triangular and hexagonal cards and cards with a hole at the center as well as holes in the corners. I see no great advantage in triangular cards, and there is a disadvantage in that the cards are harder to handle. The hexagonal cards make it possible to weave patterns with as many as six different colors, and also somewhat more elaborate figures. The fabric, too, is thicker and stiffer than that woven on square cards. The triangular and hexagonal cards may be woven in two different ways: if there is a cord through the holes at the center, one may weave one shot over the cord and back under the cord. And with the hexagonal cards, one may weave through the two-thread sheds as at (d) or through the three-thread sheds as at (e). The latter I consider the better practice.

The thread or cord through a hole at the center makes the band heavier and stronger, of course. This set-up appears to be used chiefly in the weaving of harness-bands for camels. The thread through the center does not appear on the surface of the fabric and does not add to the decorative effect.

Diagram No. 6 shows three ways of making the set-up for the more elaborate weaves, and a quick method of warping for patterns of this type. The border may be made as one pleases. For the body of the piece,

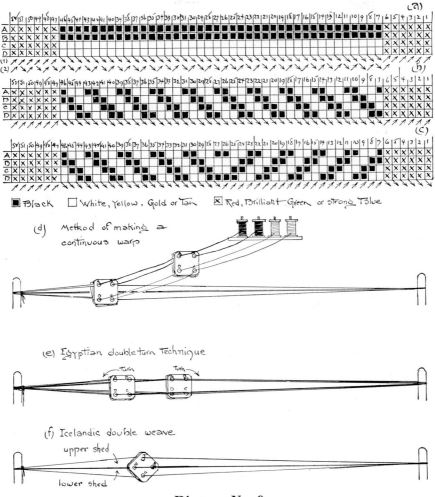

Card-Weaving — special Techniques —
Arabian, Egyptian double turn, Icelandic double weave

■ Black □ White, Yellow, Gold or Tan ☒ Red, Brilliant Green or strong Blue

(d) Method of making a continuous warp

(e) Egyptian double turn Technique

(f) Icelandic double weave
upper shed
lower shed

Diagram No. 6

as each card carries two dark threads and two light threads, the warp may be made as follows: Set up two spools of the dark-colored material and two spools of the light color on a creel of some kind. Put the cards together in a pack and draw a dark thread through all the cards at once in the hole marked A. And so with the other three threads. Attach the strand of threads to a support and draw the pack of cards along the threads to the second support, dropping off the bottom card on the way. Take the cards around the support and back to the beginning. Continue, dropping off a card from the bottom of the pack at the same place on each round till the warp is complete. If done in this manner all the cards will have the same twist, as shown by the upper row of arrows, at (1) below draft (*a*). A card may be dropped off on each side of the warp if preferred, which will give the twist shown by the lower row of arrows at (2).

The effect at (*b*) may be produced by warping as for (*a*) and then re-arranging the cards in the warp, or the cards may be arranged in the pack before the threads are drawn through the holes. This re-arrangement is shown at (*x*), **Diagram No. 7.** For patterns (*c*) and (*d*), **Diagram No. 7**—or draft (*c*), **Diagram No. 6,** arrange the cards as at (*y*), **Diagram No. 7.**

For patterns in double weave and double-faced weave the best set-up is draft (*a*), **Diagram No. 6.**

These special techniques are not simple and require a good deal of skill and practice. A beginner at card-weaving will do well to pass them by for first projects.

Of the patterns shown on **Diagram No. 7,** figures (*a*) and (*b*) are woven on the set-up at (*b*), **Diagram No. 6.** To weave pattern (*a*), turn all the cards together for four quarter-turns. Beginning at the right-hand side, slide the two cards next to the border forward till they hang in the warp ahead of the rest of the cards. The right-hand border cards may also be taken forward, which makes the following turns somewhat easier. Turn the main pack a quarter-turn forward and the right-hand group a quarter-turn in reverse, and weave. Repeat. Then slide two more cards forward, and make two turns as before. Continue in this manner till all the cards are turning in reverse. Make two quarter-turns with all the cards in this direction, and draw the pack of cards forward. Now beginning at the left-hand margin, slide two cards forward, and make two quarter-turns with the main pack in reverse and these two cards and the

Special Techniques — Borders as desired.

Finnish

Armenian

Egyptian diagonal
technique —
threading, draft
(a) (b) or (c)
diagram No.

Double-face
and double
weaves.

Patterns (a).(b)   Patterns (c).(d)

Arrangement for pattern (f)

Re-arrangements of cards threaded
as at draft (a), Diagram No. 6

Diagram No. 7

border turning forward. Continue sliding two cards forward after each
two turns till all the cards are turning forward again. This completes one
unit of the pattern, which I call "the big triangle."

A long stretch of warp is required, as the warp beyond the cards becomes twisted, and after a few figures it may become necessary to cut
the ends at (*x*) and take out the twist.

Patterns (*c*)—which we call "the big diamond"—and (*d*)—which we
call "the lotus"—are woven in the same manner on the set-up shown
at (*c*) **Diagram No. 6,** illustrated at the right-hand of **Illustration No. 1.**

Many other patterns may be woven in this technique, which seems
to me the handsomest of all the card-weaving methods.

The remaining patterns on **Diagram No. 7**—(*e*)–(*m*)—may be woven
in either the Icelandic double weave or in the Arabian double-faced
weave. For these the set-up given at (*a*), **Diagram No. 6,** is the most satisfactory. When the cards are turned all one way the result is a series of
cross-wise stripes, alternately light and dark as shown at the top of pattern (*e*). For broader stripes, weave two turns each way, first on the two
dark sheds, and then on the two light sheds. To produce the figures—the
large squares at the top of pattern (*e*), for instance—after weaving a dark
band, make a quarter-turn forward with half the cards and a quarter-
turn in reverse with the other half. Repeat. Then put all the cards together and continue by turning all the cards two quarter-turns forward
and two back, till the figures are square. Then make four turns in the
same direction, which will reverse the colors, and continue weaving two
forward and two back till the second figure is square. The other square
figures are produced in a similar manner. The position of the cards for
figure (*f*) is shown at (*z*) on the diagram.

Plain dark or plain light may be woven by turning two quarter-turns
forward and two back, continuously. As this method of weaving gives a
poor edge, the border cards may be turned continuously in one direction,
or reversed at long intervals.

To make the more elaborate figures, dark on light as sketched, weave
plain light as desired, and bring the dark color to the top as required by
the pattern in the manner described above for the square figures.

This method of weaving produces a four-ply double-faced fabric
with the same pattern on both sides with the colors reversed.

Additional patterns suitable for this weave are on **Diagram No. 7.**

For the Icelandic weave, cards are used in the position shown at (*f*), **Diagram No. 6.** There are two sheds and the weft is carried across through the upper shed and back through the lower shed each time. The set-up used is the one at (*a*), **Diagram No. 6.** To weave dark above and light below, weave first with the (A) corners of the cards on top and then with the (B) corners on top. Simply rock the cards back and forth. For the light fabric on top, weave the (C) and (D) corners in the same way. The figures are produced in a manner similar to that used for the double-faced weave. The weft should be drawn tight enough to produce a warp-faced fabric, as in other forms of card-weaving.

TRICKS IN CARD–WEAVING. Some things may be done in card-weaving that are impossible in other weaving techniques. For instance one may weave around a square corner. For this, after weaving back and forth across all the cards, weave back and forth over two less strands, omitting two cards at either the right or left margin. Continue by omitting two strands at a time till the weaving comes down to a point. Attach a stiff piece of cardboard or a small stick along the diagonal below the edge of the weaving and hang up the warp by attaching the "Y" cord to this stick. Part of the warp will be slack and it will be necessary to correct the tension, of course. Beginning at the point, weave a little wider each time till full width is regained. This is not difficult to do and the finished piece makes a handsome mounting for a picture or finish to a mat.

To weave fringes on the cards, set up a narrow band to serve as a heading, and weave this in the usual way, setting in the ready-cut fringe material as desired. The fringe material should be cut twice the length of the fringes desired, so that it may be taken through the shed, doubled and brought back through a following shed.

A card-woven finish for a bag or a runner may be made as follows: Set up a band in card-weaving of the width desired, and lay the piece to be finished on a table or shelf at right angles to the stretched warp. The piece should have long fringes of unwoven warp. Weave the cards with the warp-fringe of the piece to be finished, taking each strand back and forth at least once. The unwoven ends may be cut close after the weaving is complete.

A lengthwise slot or buttonhole may be woven in the end of a belt or girdle in card-weaving, to take the tongue of a buckle, or to permit

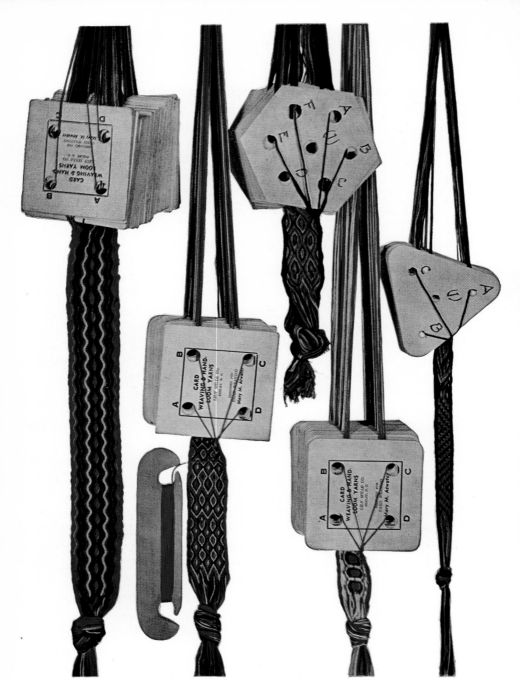

Illustration No. 2

Examples of simple card-weaving (for drafts refer to diagrams). Left to right: draft (*g*) Diagram 2; draft (*f*) Diagram 2; draft (*i*) Diagram 5; draft (*e*) Diagram 2; Ribbon of Ptahhotep, draft (*a*) Diagram 3

20

Illustration No. 3

Threading the cards

drawing through the other end of a long belt made to be worn with the end hanging down.

A piece in card-weaving may be narrowed down to a point by dropping out the cards in pairs at regular intervals—at the center or next to the border.

A technique sometimes used for belts or hatbands is to weave for a short distance in the usual way, then turn the cards without weaving, which twists together each set of four threads, for any desired distance. Then weave another bit, and so on. This produces a lively and unusual effect.

Additional oddities of technique will occur to the inventive weaver.

FINISHES. Card-woven bands may be finished in various ways. When used for belts or girdles they may be set into buckles, with or without a leather binding. Broad pieces used for belts may be woven the exact size required and finished with braided fringes, the girdle being fastened

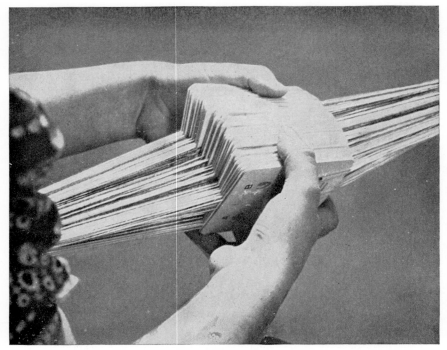

Illustration No. 4

Method of turning the cards

by tying the fringes together, as is often done with belts in Osage braid-ing. Narrow bands for belts may be woven long enough to go twice around the waist and tie, with long braided fringes. The warp being many-colored and set close, these fringes are very handsome. The best braid to use is the four-strand Indian braid. If preferred, the ends may be twisted instead of braided, but a twisted fringe does not wear as well as a braided one. Or the weaving may be brought down to a point by dropping out cards, as described above, the last threads then being drawn together and finished with a lashing to make a tassel.

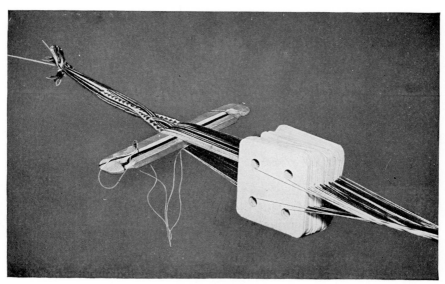

Illustration No. 5

Card-weaving set-up in weaving position. Pattern shown is the braided
pattern, draft *(i–j)* Diagram 2

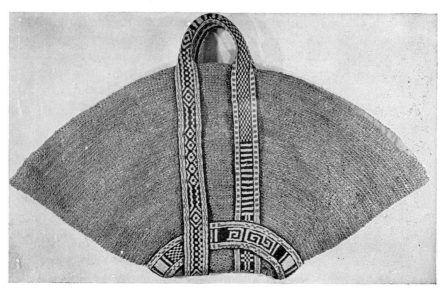

Illustration No. 6

A card-woven band used as handles for a bag in crocheted raffia

PART II

—— "Inkles" and the Inkle Loom ——

ACCORDING to Webster (unabridged) an "inkle" is "a kind of linen tape or braid"—though exactly what kind is not revealed. It follows logically enough that an "inkle loom" is a contrivance on which narrow bands may be woven. Such a loom, used in days of old in England, is illustrated at (a), **Diagram No. 8.** It was used for the making of "galluses," garter bands, draw-strings, and so on. A somewhat similar loom, but a bit more elaborate and operated by a foot-treadle, is shown in Scandinavian books on weaving.

As far as I have been able to discover, there were no inkle looms in the cargo of the *Mayflower,* and I think the first one to reach the United States was probably the one sent me some years ago from England sketched at (a), **Diagram No. 8.** Inkle weaving in the colonies appears to have been done on the so-called "lap loom," or hole-and-slot heddle shown at (c) on **Diagram No. 8.**

The hole-and-slot heddle is a very ancient form of loom and is used by the Indians of our Southwest and by the native weavers of the Philippines as well as in the European countries.

A modern version of the inkle loom designed by E. E. Gilmore of Stockton, California, is sketched at (d) on the diagram. This is more convenient to weave upon than either the old English floor model or the heddle.

Though woven linen galluses and garter bands are now as extinct as the fabulous dodo, we of today have many uses for narrow fabrics, as noted in the previous section. Though such bands may of course be woven on a large treadle loom if one chooses, it is pleasant to produce them on the inkle loom. One may "inkle" agreeably while listening to the radio, during conversational interludes, out-of-doors on the porch or in

Equipment used in "Inkle" Weaving

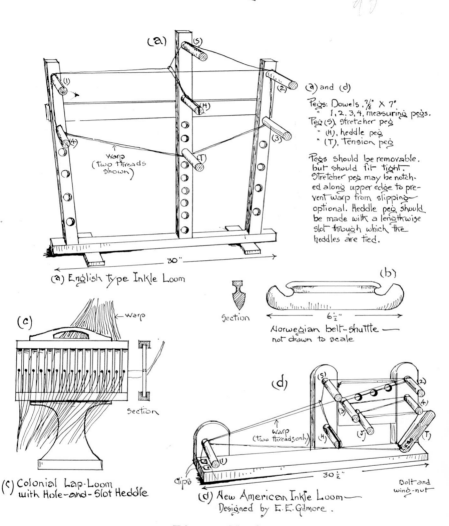

(a) and (d)

Pegs: Dowels .⅞" X 7".
  " 1, 2, 3, 4, measuring pegs.
Peg (S), Stretcher peg
  " (H), heddle peg
  " (T), Tension peg

Pegs should be removable,
but should fit tight.
Stretcher peg may be notched along upper edge to prevent warp from slipping —
optional. Heddle peg should
be made with a lengthwise
slot through which the
heddles are tied.

(a) English type Inkle Loom

(b)

Section   Norwegian belt-shuttle —
             not drawn to scale

6½"

(c) Colonial Lap-Loom
with Hole-and-Slot Heddle

(d) New American Inkle Loom —
Designed by E. E. Gilmore.

Diagram No. 8

the garden, at camp, even during long trips by train or boat, as the loom is small and easily portable, and weaving upon it is noiseless.

Weaving on the inkle loom, be it understood, is not a time-wasting and yarn-wasting pastime such as some of the "weaving" done on small contraptions of one kind and another that one finds in the shops—and sometimes, alas! in the schools. It is a special kind of weaving, entirely practical and as technical as weaving on a large loom, though of course limited. I find a width of four inches about the practical extreme.

EQUIPMENT.   At first glance, the inkle loom appears to be simply a small warping frame equipped with a simple shedding attachment that permits weaving off the warp directly from the frame. And in essence that is what it is. Any carpenter or anyone handy with wood-working tools will find it simple enough to build one of these affairs. But please note that the construction should not be flimsy. A stretched warp—even one only a few inches wide—exerts more pull than one might imagine, and the thing must be sturdy to keep the pegs in alignment. Exact proportions are unimportant, however. In the English model at (*a*) on the diagram, the distance from the base to peg No. 1 should suit the convenience of the weaver as seated at the end of the loom. The pegs should be ¾″ dowels, 7″ long, and should fit tight in the holes but should be removable —except pegs (1) and (2), which may be fixed if desired.

The little Norwegian belt-shuttle, sketched at (*b*) on the diagram, and mentioned also in the previous section, is a desirable piece of equipment for inkle-weaving, though any type of small shuttle may be used.

TYPES OF INKLE–WEAVING.   The directions received with the first inkle loom sent me from England dealt only with plain weaving, with the suggestion that the woven bands might later be decorated with embroidery. This seemed to me of limited interest, though it is true that many handsome pattern effects may be produced in the plain weave by the arrangements of colors in the warp—as in the drafts shown on **Diagram No. 9.** However, it soon occurred to me that the Indian belt-weaves produced on the hole-and-slot heddle might be woven more conveniently on the inkle loom, as might also the more elaborate belt-weaves of Guatemala, Mexico, Peru and other countries, produced as a rule on the prehistoric body loom. I shall describe these interesting techniques.

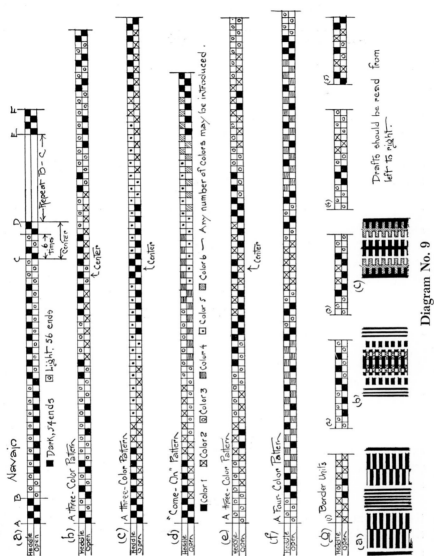

Diagram No. 9

MATERIALS. Though Webster specifies linen as the material for inkle-weaving, modern inklers use a wide variety of materials, from coarse to fine, in cotton, wool or worsted, silk, nylon, and rayon, as well as linen. Moreover different materials may be combined in the same piece. As most of the fabrics are of the warp-face structure, the materials used for warp should be handsome and colorful as a rule. The weft—usually coarser than the warp—is completely covered and does not appear in most of these weaves. For belts where stiffness is desirable, the weft should be a hard, stiff material, such as a hard-twisted coarse linen. Ordinary carpet warp serves well as weft material for many weaves. Soft and fuzzy materials are undesirable for either warp or weft.

SETTING UP THE LOOM. The processes of warping and threading are carried out at the same time in setting up the inkle loom. So a word here about the drafts. I have written the drafts to be read from left to right, as this is the way the threading is done. In each pair of warp-ends, one thread is taken around the pegs of the frame as on any warping board except that no lease is made. The second thread is taken over the same course but between the pegs numbered (1) and (2) it is taken through a heddle and over the notched peg above it. The lower row of the drafts shows the threads taken plain through the loom and the upper row shows the threads taken through heddles. Colors are indicated by the hatchings.

The length of the warp—up to the capacity of the loom—is controlled by the manner in which the pegs are set and the warp is taken around them. The sketch at (a), **Diagram No. 8,** shows the shortest warp that may be made on the English type of inkle loom, and the sketch at (d) shows the longest warp that may be set up on the table type loom. The peg marked (T) on the sketch at (a), **Diagram No. 8,** and the wooden slab marked (t) on the sketch at (d), provide the tension.

Begin by attaching the end of the first thread to peg (1), making the tie with a bow-knot so that it may be untied easily. Or on loom (d) slip the end under one of the metal clips under peg (1). Take the thread over and under the pegs to produce the length of warp desired, and back under peg (1). For the second thread, take the warp-end over peg (1), through the first heddle, over the notched stretcher peg, over peg (2) and around the remaining pegs in the same way as with thread 1. Proceed in this manner for the entire warp, alternating an "open" thread with a thread through a heddle and over the stretcher peg, observing, of course, the changes of color as shown by the draft being used.

After a number of threads have been warped—the exact number does not matter—cut the warp-end a few inches beyond peg (1); release the tie made around the peg at the start and tie the two ends together. As the endless warp travels around the pegs during weaving, it must not be left anchored to the peg.

Care must be taken to warp all threads at an even tension. There is a tendency to make the last part of the warp tighter than the first part, and if this happens, the weaving will be crooked.

As noted above, the weft material used may be anything one chooses, and in any color, as it is covered by the warp and does not show—except along the edges. It is good practice to warp four threads on either edge in the color of the weft to be used.

WEAVING.   To weave, take a position at the left-hand end of the loom. To make the first shed, insert the hand between the upper and lower parts of the warp, behind the heddles, and press down. This will open a shed in front of the heddles through which the shuttle will pass. For the second shed, lift the lower threads, behind the heddles, as shown on **Diagram No. 10.**

As the inkle loom has no reed or batten, the width of the fabric must be controlled by the weft, and the density of the fabric by the manner in which the weft is beaten close, either with the edge of the shuttle or with the ends of the fingers, or with a comb, or with a knife inserted in the shed. As most inkle fabrics are of the warp-face type, the weft should be drawn close enough to bring the warp closely together over the weft. And for most fabrics the weft should be driven together as firmly as possible. It is important to keep an even width and Indian weavers sometimes use a little "template" consisting of a stick or slip of wood with small brads set the desired distance apart. This is not, however, strictly necessary.

As the take-up is all in the warp, the warp should not be stretched very tight, and the tension should be released from time to time as weaving progresses. Otherwise it will become impossible to drive the weft close together and the work will tend to narrow in.

When the weaving has come close to the heddles the tension should be released and the warp pulled forward as required.

For the plain weave the above directions are all that may be required. If the warp is all of one color, a plain colored tape in warp-faced rep will be the result, but as such a tape is not very handsome it is the usual practice to produce pattern effects by using several colors in the warp. It is interesting to note that a great many varied effects may be achieved.

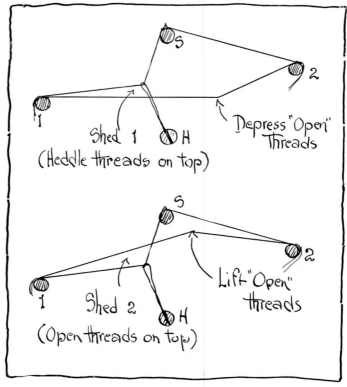

Shed 1   H
(Heddle threads on top)

Depress "Open" Threads

Shed 2   H
(Open threads on top)

Lift "Open" threads

Diagram No. 10

A few patterns of this type are shown on **Diagram No. 9,** and the woven result of several of these patterns is shown on **Illustration No. 7.** The pattern at (*a*) is Navajo, done in a hard-twisted wool yarn in natural and grey. Of course any two contrasting colors might be used. The pattern at (*d*), which I call the "Come-On" pattern, is always a good choice for a first adventure in inkle weaving as it is so gay and so simple to weave. Even a small child or a very timid beginning weaver finds it delightful. A set-up in perle cotton #5 is suggested. A similar pattern, from Guatemala, is given below. The complete set-up as given makes a wide band but of course only a part of it may be used if desired. This piece was woven with two kinds of weft—a coarse and a fine, as follows: fine, coarse, fine, coarse, fine, fine, coarse, fine, coarse, fine, and repeat. This brings two fine shots together after each five shots and produces an interesting variation in texture. The weft material should be in dark blue, as the edges are in this color. If a white weft is preferred, the four outer threads on each edge should be set up in white.

A GUATEMALAN GIRDLE IN PLAIN WEAVE

Threaded as for plain weave. Arrangement of colors as follows:

20 ends, dark blue	8 "	white, purple, alternately
6 ends, red, purple alternately	8 "	purple, white, "
6 " purple, red, "	14 "	dark blue
8 ends dark blue	8 "	gold, grey, alternately
8 " red, mauve, alternately	8 "	grey, gold, "
8 " mauve, red, "	14 "	dark blue
8 ends dark blue	10 "	green, rose, alternately
10 ends, red, white, alternately	10 "	rose, green, "
10 " white, red "	14 "	dark blue
12 ends dark blue	8 "	red, purple, alternately
8 " green, purple, alternately	8 "	purple, red, "
8 " purple, green "	14 ends dark blue
10 " dark blue	8 "	white, grey, alternately
8 " gold, grey, alternately	8 "	grey, white,
8 " grey, gold, "	14 ends dark blue
14 " dark blue	8 "	red, gold, alternately
8 " red and purple, alternately	8 "	gold, red, "
8 " purple, red, "	14 ends dark blue
14 " dark blue	10 ends gold, grey, alternately
8 " white, purple, alternately	10 "	grey, gold, "
8 " purple, white "	14 "	dark blue
14 " dark blue	8 ends red, white, alternately
8 " red, mauve, alternately	8 "	white, red, "
8 " mauve, red, "	14 ends dark blue
14 ends dark blue	8 ends gold, mauve, alternately
8 " red, gold, alternately	8 "	mauve, gold, "
8 " gold, red, alternately	20 ends dark blue.
14 " dark blue		

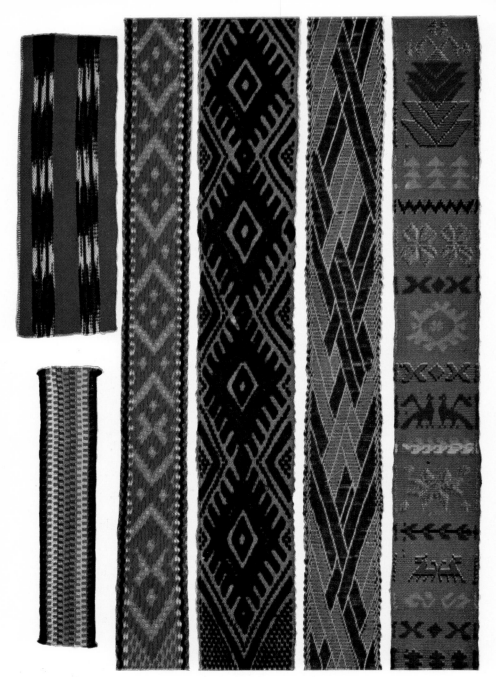

Illustration No. 7

Inkles. Left to right: upper, plain weave with stripes in tie-dyed yarn; lower, plain weave, draft (*d*) Diagram 9; Finnish pattern, draft (*b*) Diagram 14; Central European, draft (*c*) Diagram 14; Peruvian, draft (*c*) Diagram 15; Mexican, draft (*a*) Diagram 15

PICK–UP PATTERNS. The most interesting weaves for the inkle loom are, however, the various pick-up techniques. The simplest of these is a "native" American weave found in pieces from Bolivia and Guatemala. As a rule, these are done in black and white or black and natural, with a border—wide or narrow as desired—in either bright red or a vivid green. For the pattern part of the piece the warp is alternately black and white,

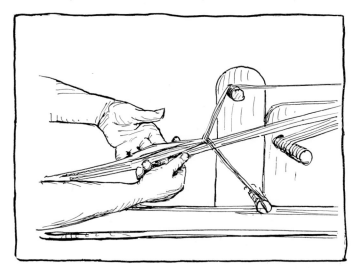

Diagram No. 11

with all the black threads warped "open" and all the white threads through heddles, as shown on **Diagram No. 12.**

Diagram No. 11 shows the position of the hands in making the pick-up. Open the desired shed and insert the left hand. Beginning at the right-hand margin, pick up the desired threads with the right hand, taking up also the raised threads and slipping the right hand along till the left-hand edge is reached and the new shed is on the right hand. Insert the shuttle and weave. A little practice makes this quick and easy.

All the (*a*) patterns on **Diagram No. 12** are woven in the same manner: Weave the "up" shed plain and make the pick-up on the "down" shed. I find it convenient to weave the up-shed from left to right, and the down-shed from right to left.

In detail, to weave the figure at (*a-5*) which—believe it or not, repre-

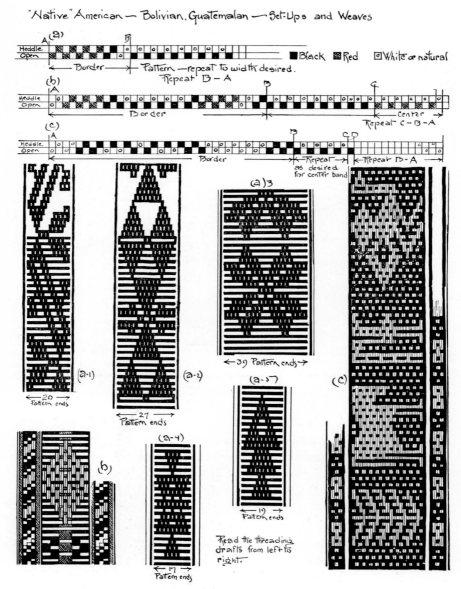

"Native" American — Bolivian, Guatemalan — Set-Ups and Weaves

■ Black   ▨ Red   □ White or natural

Read the threading drafts from left to right.

Diagram No. 12

sents a fish and stands for good fortune—weave the raised shed which makes the black bar all across. Change the shed and hold it on the left hand as described. Take the right hand through the shed as far as the

Illustration No. 8

English type of inkle loom set up to a short warp, with sample inkles

sixth of the black threads, which pick up. Go under the next two white threads and pick up the eighth black thread. Under two white threads again, and pick up the tenth black thread, and so on till five black threads have been picked up. Take the right hand the rest of the way through the shed and weave. Weave the raised shed plain. On the next down-shed, pick up the seventh black thread, go under the next two white threads and pick up the ninth black thread, and so on till four black threads

"Native" American—Mexican, Navajo, Zuñi, etc.

(a) Navajo
(b) Mexican "Tree" motif
(c)   "   "War Dance
(d) Philippine "Snake-and-Egg" motif
(e) Peruvian motif
(f) Mexican "Winged Serpent"

Diagram No. 13

have been taken up. Continue in the same manner till the figure is complete. All patterns of this type are woven in the same manner. A woven piece on pattern (*a-2*) is shown on **Illustration No. 8.**

Pattern (*b*) is also a Bolivian pattern with a border design and a band of red through the center of the pattern stripe. One figure is picked up in white pairs as shown on the sketch, and the smaller figure is picked up in black pairs. For pattern (*c*), the figures are picked up in white pairs and the background in single black threads. This is also a Bolivian pattern.

The set-up for the patterns on **Diagram No. 13** is similar to that on **Diagram No. 12,** except that the figures are all woven in the dark color—usually a dark blue—on a white or natural ground. The dark threads should be much coarser than the light threads, or may be double threads as shown on the diagram. Borders, again, are usually in bright red or a vivid green. This is a typical Mexican belt-weave, and similar pieces may be found among the Navajos and other Indians of the Southwest. It is a very handsome weave—so handsome, in fact, that I was led to translate it into a form that may be woven on a four-harness treadle loom, and as wide as one may wish. In this form it is an excellent weave for a variety of purposes. Directions will be found in my "Shuttle-craft Book," revised edition, pages 318–21.

As woven on the inkle loom: For the background effect weave the down-shed plain, and on the up-shed weave under alternate dark threads. Weave the following down-shed plain, and on the next up-shed, weave under alternate dark threads again—the threads skipped on the first up-shed. For the solid dark effect, weave the up-shed plain, and on the down-shed pick up alternating dark threads. For the figures, combine these two methods, as indicated clearly (I hope!) on the drawings. Woven pieces in this weave are shown on **Illustration No. 8.**

This is not a true warp-faced weave as the weft shows across the background areas as a fine criss-cross pattern, very attractive in effect. The weft should not be drawn tight enough to spoil this texture. Bands in this weave are therefore wider than those with the same number of warp-ends done in the previously described weave.

Diagram No. 14 shows the set-up used in Europe for weavings of the inkle type—usually woven, to be sure, on the hole-and-slot heddle.

When woven in plain weave, this form of set-up produces a dotted effect as shown at the bottom of the Finnish pattern at (*b*), and pick-ups

'Staggered' Set-Up,—Mexican and European

(a) A   Mexican   B   C

Repeat A–C, four times. Repeat B–A

⊡ White, fine   ▨ Red, fine   ■ Dark blue, coarse

(b) A Finnish   B   C

←——— Border ———→ ←— 5 times —→   Repeat B–A

(c) A Europeαn B   C

←— Repeat —→ ←— End —→
   20 times

(d) | Border I

May be used with any pattern
and woven without pick-up.

(e) | Border II

May be used with any pattern and
woven without pick-up

(c) Central Europeαn   (b) Finnish

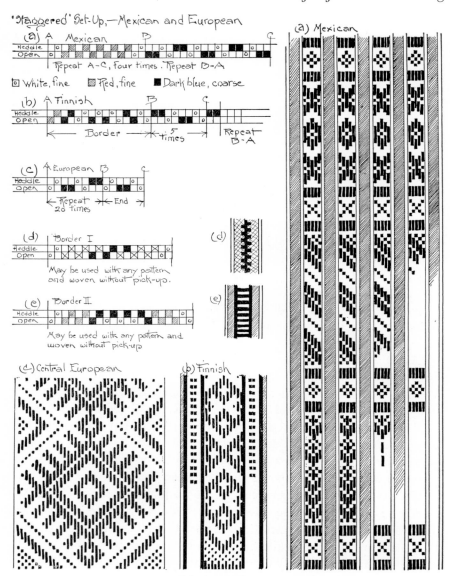

Diagram No. 14

are made on each shed. Moreover part of the pattern effect is in "push-down" rather than in pick-up. An entirely different set of effects results.

A similar set-up may be used for a Mexican weave shown at (a). In this, colored stripes—usually in bright red—in plain weave, alternate with narrow pattern stripes in white, each with five heavy or doubled pattern threads in dark blue.

The Finnish ski-belt from which pattern (b) was written had a plain-weave border in black and yellow with a pattern band in orange for the single background threads, and bright red for the doubled pattern threads. The material was a coarse knitting worsted.

To weave this pattern, begin with several shots in plain weave. To make the figure, weave the shot that brings up the middle thread. On the next shot, pick up the middle thread, which will be down. On the following shot, pick up a thread on each side of the middle thread. On the next shed, pick up the second thread from the center on each side and suppress the middle thread which comes up again on this shed. Continue in this manner, picking up and pushing down threads, as required by the pattern. In general, a thread is picked up only once, which makes a three-thread skip. Sometimes, however, a longer skip may be allowed, as in several places in this pattern. The technique is simple.

For the Mexican pattern shown at (a), the manner of weaving is exactly the same. Each change of figure is woven on each of the bands for a distance of a few inches before changing. It is amazing to find how many changes are possible on the five threads composing the patterns.

The techniques shown on **Diagram No. 15** are similar in method though different in effect. The technique at (a) is Mexican and is also occasionally seen in pieces from Guatemala. For the patterns at (a), set the warp in fine material in a plain color—white or natural or any other light color—with two or four ends in a contrasting color set a few threads from the edge on either side. Sometimes a very fine warp is used, warped double—two ends open and two ends through the heddle—all across. The foundation fabric is a warp-faced rep, but the figures are in skips of colored weft. The weft should be a good deal coarser than the warp. In weaving, open a shed and weave a shot of foundation weft. With the shed still open, make a pick-up for the pattern weft, using a small pick-up stick, and taking the pattern weft between the colored edge threads only. When firmly beaten up, the pattern weft lies over the foundation weft,

"Native" American, Mexican, Peruvian.
Weft Pattern Techniques.

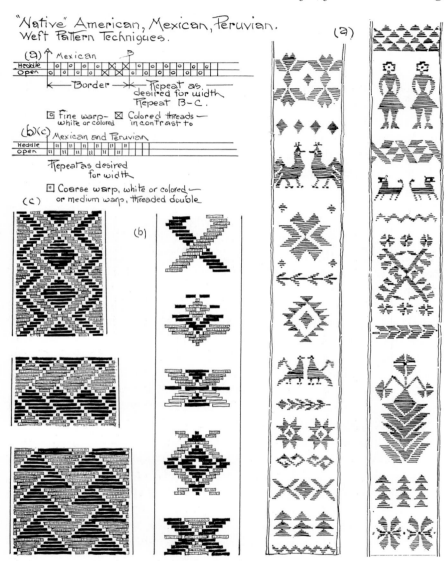

(a) Mexican

Heddle	o	o	o	o	o	o	X	X	o	o	o	o	o	o	o
Open	o	o	o	o	o	o	X	X	o	o	o	o	o	o	o

|←——— Border ———→|←— Repeat as desired for width Repeat B-C.

⊡ Fine warp– white or colored   ⊠ Colored threads – in contrast to

(b)(c) Mexican and Peruvian

Heddle		ll		ll		ll		ll		ll		
Open	ll		ll		ll		ll		ll			

Repeat as desired for width

Ⅲ Coarse warp, white or colored – or medium warp, threaded double

(c)

(b)

(a)

Diagram No. 15

and the warp is close enough to cover it over the background spaces. It is, of course, these background spaces that should be taken up on the pick-up stick.

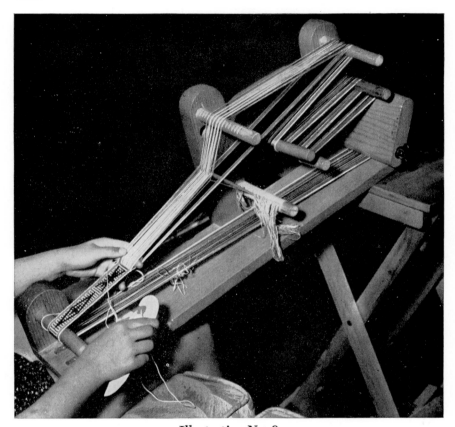

Illustration No. 9

Weaving on the inkle loom

The little figures may be woven in a variety of colors and the effect is very lively and amusing. The pattern weft does not show at all on the reverse side of the fabric, which presents the appearance of a plain-colored rep.

The weave at (*b*) is similar, except that much coarser material is used for both warp and weft, and the figures are woven in two colors

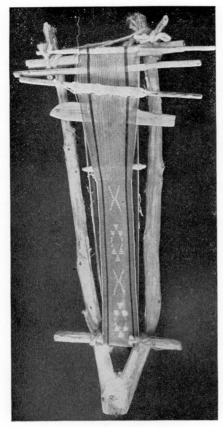

Illustration No. 10

Navajo belt loom. Technique of weave as given on Diagram 13. American Museum of Natural History, New York, N. Y.

with an outline in warp between the various parts of the figures. Open the shed and weave a shot of foundation weft. With the shed still open, make a pick-up for the first color, and weave. Still with the same shed open, make a pick-up for the second color, and weave. In this weave, the weft shows a little across the background as usually woven.

The weave at (*c*) is also done over a coarse warp. Two colors are used in the weft and the surface of the fabric is completely covered by skips of weft. In producing this weave, I find it best to use two small pick-up sticks. Open the shed and on the first stick take up the outline threads. On the second stick, make the pick-up for the first color, and weave. Take out the second stick, but with the same shed open and the first stick still in position, make the pick-up for the second color, and weave. No foundation shot is required as one of the colors tabbies where the other color skips.

This is a very handsome weave and may also be produced on a two-harness loom, or on any threading that gives the two tabby sheds —as described in my "Shuttle-craft Book," revised edition, pages 301–305. It is a weave for coarse material, however, and is not suitable for fine materials.

PART III

Twined Weaving

Twined weaving is so ancient that it may be said to have no history. It is found in many parts of the world, as remote from each other as the South Seas, Persia, the Subarctic, in somewhat varying forms, and used for widely different purposes. Among modern American weavers it is virtually unknown, though it might well be used more freely, as it offers interesting possibilities.

EQUIPMENT.   When a Maori woman of the South Seas decides to make herself a "taniko" headband, a grass skirt or a shaggy rain-cape she finds herself a pleasant spot out-of-doors and drives two stout stakes into the ground, a suitable distance apart. She twists two cords together and stretches them between the stakes, and sitting upon the ground between the stakes, she proceeds to weave.

We may do likewise if we choose, but as most of us prefer—for prolonged sitting—a chair or a bench to the open ground, we may use a frame of some sort or, if out-of-doors, two suitably placed trees, or two porch-pillars. An old picture-frame will serve, if it is large enough and solid enough, or an old-fashioned embroidery-frame may be used. If a specially constructed frame is preferred, it is an advantage to have the uprights lightly notched along the outer edges as this helps to keep the work in place. No other equipment is required.

MATERIAL.   The warp for the Maori forms of twined weaving should be coarse and stiff. For the taniko technique it should also be smooth. In the taniko headband from New Zealand shown on **Illustration No. 11,** the pattern of which is given in detail at (c) and (d), **Diagram No. 17,** the warp is a very coarse black linen such as is used in sewing heavy

43

Maori Weaving

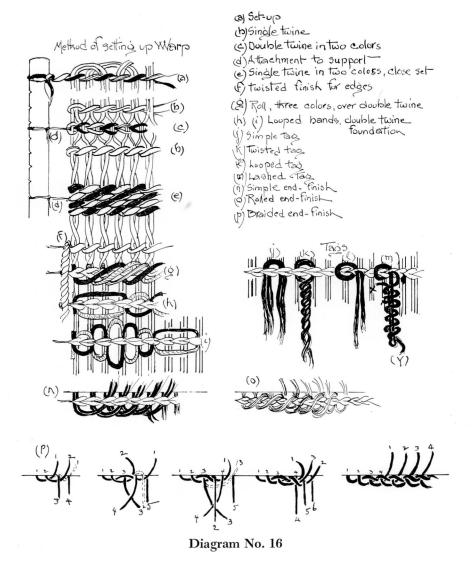

Method of setting up Warp

(a)
(b)
(c)
(d)
(h)
(d)
(e)
(f)
(g)
(h)
(c)
(n)

(a) Set-up
(b) Single twine
(c) Double twine in two colors
(d) Attachment to support
(e) Single twine in two colors, close set
(f) twisted finish for edges

(g) Roll, three colors, over double twine
(h) (i) Looped bands, double twine foundation
(j) Simple Tag
(k) Twisted tag
(l) looped tag
(m) Lashed Tag
(n) Simple end-finish
(o) Rolled end-finish
(p) Braided end-finish

Tags
(j)   (k)   (l)   (m)

(Y)

(o)

(P)

Diagram No. 16

boots. The weft material in this piece is a fine, soft silk in many colors.
For bags, table mats and the like I have found a lightweight jute makes
an excellent warp. Macramé cord may also be used for the purpose. Wool
is not a desirable weft material, but coarse cottons, rayons, silks—even
raffia—may be used with good results.

Native Maori fabrics are often decorated with interwoven feathers,
tufts of dog-hair and "tags" of various kinds. Several forms of tag are
illustrated on **Diagram No. 16.**

WARP SET–UP. For such pieces as belts and headbands the warp
runs the narrow way of the piece. It should be measured off and cut in
pieces a little more than twice the length required, to allow for the
braided finish. The manner of making the set-up is illustrated at (*a*) on
the diagram. Two cords twisted together and stretched between the two
uprights—whatever they may be—form the loom and are the foundation
for the warp. Beginning at the left-hand edge of the proposed warp, draw
apart the two strands of the twist and insert a pair of warp-ends, drawing
them through half-way. Take a second pair of warp-ends through the
second twist of the foundation cord. Through the next twist bring the
first pair down. Continue by alternately drawing a new pair through the
twist and bringing the last pair down till the warp is complete. The warp
is permitted to hang free from the foundation cord. This set-up is shown
at (*a*), **Diagram No. 16.**

WEAVING. The fabric is produced by twining, somewhat like basketry,
beginning always at the left and continued toward the right, the twining
being done over pairs of warp-ends. Sometimes a pair of weft-ends is used
and sometimes a double twining is made with two pairs of weft-ends, as
illustrated. If an open effect is desired, the pairs of warp-ends should be
split as between rows (*b*), (*c*) and (*d*) on the diagram. If a solid effect is
desired successive rows of twining should be made over the same pairs
each time, as at (*e*). A rippled effect may be produced by twisting the
warp-ends between the rows as shown between (*b*) and (*e*) and between (*e*) and (*f*) on the diagram. These processes are very simple, but
should be carried out with exactness, and the warp should be coarse
enough and set close enough together to hold the weft twists securely.
When the right-hand edge is reached, the weft-ends may be twined back

Maori Taniko Weaving

(a)

(b)

(c)

(e)

Face

Foundation
strand

Reverse
(f)

(a), (b) Typical patterns

(c) Center figure of head-band
    shown on illustration

(d) End figure of head-band
    (left hand)

(x) Points of joining.

■ Black ▨ Red ▣ Orange □ White
Colors in head-band

(x)   (d)   (x)

Diagram No. 17

under the last few warp-ends and cut off, or the ends may be left loose to be finished later with a needle.

Another method of making a finished edge is shown at (f) on the diagram. A twist of two or more ends is carried along each edge to hold the weft-ends.

To keep the fabric from narrowing in as the work progresses, it is wise to make an occasional attachment to the uprights as shown at (*d*) on the diagram.

Various forms of decoration may be introduced as sketched at (*g*), (*h*) and (*i*) on the diagram. The roll at (*g*) is particularly effective. It is made over a plain double twining as shown on the illustration. Three strands of coarse material in different colors are used for the roll. Four or more strands may also be used but three strands seem to give the best effect. Begin by taking the end of the first colored strand down through a loop of the twining. Attach the second and third strands in the same manner. When the fourth loop of the twining is reached, bring the first strand of the roll up across the other two strands and down through the loop. Continue in the same manner with each strand in succession all across. The roll is sketched in open form for the sake of clearness, but the effect is better if the strands are drawn fairly close as made. The manner of producing the ornamental effects at (*h*) and (*i*) is so clearly shown on the diagram that it needs no description.

"Tags" are a prominent feature of Maori weaving—sometimes used as decoration, set at intervals, and sometimes set close as in the case of rain-capes. Several types of tag are shown at (*j*), (*k*), (*l*) and (*m*) on the diagram. The simple attachment at (*j*) is not very practical as it tends to pull out, but when the two strands of inserted material are twisted as at (*k*) the result is better. The attachment at (*l*) is firm, also. The tag at (*m*) is similar to a sailor's lashing. One of the ends is doubled back to form a loop and the other end is then twisted around the doubled end. In the sketch, the wrapping is shown loose, for the sake of clearness, but should be drawn tight. When the wrapping is complete, the end of the wrapping cord—(*y*) on the diagram—should be slipped through the loop of the first cord—(*x*)—which should then be drawn tight. The ends may then be clipped close.

At (*n*), (*o*) and (*p*), are shown methods of finishing off the warp-ends. These should be carried out on the "wrong" side of the piece. The finish at (*n*) consists of a double twine through which the warp-ends are brought up and secured. It may tend to pull out and the similar form at (*o*) is better. The preferred finish, however, is the braid at (*p*)—known as the "two up and two down" braid. The series of sketches will, it is hoped, make the process clear. After the motion is acquired, this braid

Illustration No. 11

Upper: Maori headband in taniko weaving. In silks over a coarse black linen warp. Lower: bag in Maori-type twining. Bottom in taniko. Handle and binding, card-weaving

48

may be made rapidly and easily. If the warp is coarse and stiff, as it should be for twined weaving, and the "tucks" of the braid are drawn tight, this makes an excellent finish, used on most taniko pieces. The ends, however, should not be clipped too short. They are covered by the lining ordinarily used on such pieces.

The taniko technique is the high art of Maori twined weaving. The warp for this should be set up in single ends and should be set as close as possible. A foundation cord should then be stretched between the loom uprights, behind the warp, together with a strand of colored weft material including a yarn of each of the colors to be used in the proposed design. The twining is then carried out as shown at (*e*) and (*f*), **Diagram No. 17.** Beginning at the left, the weft strand of the first color of the pattern is brought up at a slant across the first warp-end, then down behind the foundation strand and the other colored strands, up between threads 1 and 2 of the warp and upward at a slant across thread 2, and so on for the number of tucks required by the design. The figures of the patterns are produced by making changes of color. The method of twining remains the same throughout.

The effect of this technique is surprisingly similar to petit-point embroidery, and taniko pieces might be used for chair-seats and similar pieces, and elaborate patterns might be developed. The typical Maori patterns, however, are simple and geometric, made up for the most part of big and little triangles. Traditionally the background is always black no matter what colors are used for the designs.

Illustration No. 11 shows a Maori headband sent me from New Zealand. Also a bag made by me—over a warp of fine jute—showing a number of the Maori twinings with taniko at the bottom of the piece. **Illustrations 12** and **13** show groups of Maori dancers wearing taniko headbands and taniko weaving for bodices and skirt-hems.

For further information on Maori twined weaving see "The Evolution of Maori Clothing," by Te Rangi Hiroa (Peter H. Buck).

PUEBLO AND OJIBWA TWINED WEAVING. The Hopi and Zuni Indians of Arizona and New Mexico practice twined weaving in various forms—most commonly for large mats of twisted fibers and also for an interesting form of blanket made of rabbit fur. For the latter the rabbit skins are cut in strips about a quarter of an inch wide and made into a

Illustration No. 12

Maori dancing girls. Bodices and hems of skirts in taniko weaving

Illustration No. 13

Maori dancing girls. Headbands and bodices in taniko weaving

Illustration No. 14

Set-up and start of a table mat in simple Maori twined weaving

coarse yarn by twisting around a fiber cord. This yarn is used as warp and the twining is done in fiber, the rows being set some distance apart. Sometimes feathers are used in the same manner.

The Ojibwa (Chippewa) Indians of Minnesota and Michigan use twined weaving for the making of food-bags. The twisted cords of the warp-foundation are tied to make a ring and this is taken around two uprights. The twining is done in endless fashion, around and around, till the desired length is reached. The top of the piece of weaving becomes the bottom of the bag, the foundation cords being seamed together, and the top of the bag is finished in plaiting to provide openings for a draw-string.

CHILCAT TWINED WEAVING.   The Chilcat blankets of the far north are rarely seen except in museums. I had been told that they were no longer being made and that the technique was a so-called "lost art" among the Indian women of that region. However I recently had the interesting experience of seeing one of these pieces under construction. The Indian weaver was not, to be sure, using the traditional warp of twisted cedar-bark fibers and was using a fine worsted yarn for weft instead of the spun goat-hair of the ancient pieces, but the method and the patterns were strictly according to ancient tribal tradition.

The set-up—of free-hanging warp attached to a twisted foundation cord stretched between two uprights—was the same as for Maori weaving, and the twining was done in a similar manner, but the effect was entirely different. The twining was done back and forth across single areas of the pattern, instead of being woven from left to right all across the piece on each successive row; and the rows of twining were pushed close together to make a solid fabric similar to tapestry in effect. Where perpendicular lines occurred, the rows of adjoining areas were sometimes interlocked around a single warp-end and sometimes left as slits to be sewed together.

The colors used in these pieces are usually black, white, yellow and green; and the patterns usually consist of a highly stylized bear's head seen full face, and beaked profiles of the thunder-bird. A handsome example from the American Museum of Natural History in New York is shown on **Illustration No. 15.**

It seems unlikely that many weavers will feel an urge to make a Chil-cat blanket of traditional form, but the technique is of interest and might be used for entirely different purposes and in different patterns.

These pieces, be it noted, are not "blankets" in the usual meaning of the word, but are actually capes, worn about the shoulders. The long fringes are purely decorative and are made separately of wool and ap-plied to the finished weaving and are not made of warp-ends.

A PERSIAN SADDLE–BAG.   I recently had an opportunity to examine in detail an interesting and beautiful piece of twined weaving from Persia

Illustration No. 15

Chilcat blanket. American Museum of Natural History, New York, N. Y.

—or Iran, if one prefers. It was woven of very fine mohair yarns in dull red, natural white, dark blue, brown and rose over a warp of fine natural linen set at 30 ends to the inch, used double, giving an actual setting of 15 ends to the inch.

The body of the piece was a plain rep woven in the dull red color, and the set-up was probably made on a tapestry loom of some kind with the warp held at both ends, the rep not being in twining and probably woven with a shuttle.

The piece was ornamented with ten decorative bands separated by the bands of plain rep. These bands were in twined weaving, and the patterns are shown in detail on **Diagram No. 18.**

The twining, as in the Chilcat blanket, was pressed close to make a solid fabric resembling tapestry, or soumak; but unlike the Chilcat tech-

A Persian Saddle-Bag

Stripes 1 and 9

Stripes 2, 4, 6, 8

Figures: dark blue, white, dark blue, rose. Background, brown

Stripes 3, 7.

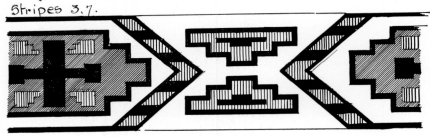

Stripe 5

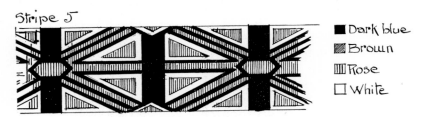

■ Dark blue
▨ Brown
▥ Rose
□ White

Stripe 10

Diagram No. 18

nique, the rows of twining appeared to be carried all across instead of back and forth, the colored weft threads not in use being allowed to lie at the back in long floats. The piece was lined to cover these floats.

The making of so fine a piece in this technique would be a long and arduous job, and it seems unlikely that many weavers would care to attempt it, even though the results are unusually handsome. However the patterns and the technique might be used for pieces in coarser material and for other purposes. Any one of these bands, for instance, would make a handsome belt. The work would be easier and more rapid if made on a set-up with a free warp as in Maori and Chilcat twining, rather than on a warp attached at both ends.

PART IV

———— Braiding and Knotting ————

THERE is no intention to treat exhaustively here of the arts of braiding and knotting. A considerable literature on the subject is available and there is little value in the repetition of material that may be obtained elsewhere. I should like to mention a book that, in my opinion, should be in every weaver's library, and that would be useful to many craftsmen and others who are not weavers. This is: "The Encyclopedia of Knots and Fancy Rope-Work" by Raoul Graumont and John Hensel. These two accomplished sailormen have given in highly usable form all—one might think—that any sane person needs in the way of braids and knots, including some of the most extravagantly hideous examples of macramé imaginable.

However there are a number of interesting and useful braids that never went to sea, so here are some of them.

The four-strand braid at (a), **Diagram No. 19,** is a very useful braid— used for the handsome long fringes of braided belts, such as the ones in Osage braiding. It is useful for fringes made on any close-set warp, particularly a warp in several colors. It is a simple braid and after one acquires the special motion it can be made as rapidly as an ordinary three-strand braid.

If the material is in two colors, as shown on the sketch, use two strands of each color. These may be single strands or, in fine material, strands made up of several single ends. Hold the two strands of one color in the right hand and the strands of the other color in the left. Take the outside strand on the right behind the braid, up between the two opposite strands and back across one of the left-hand strands to the right. Now take the outer strand on the left back behind the braid and up between the two strands on the right. Then across a single right-

56

A Group of Useful Braids and Coxcombs.

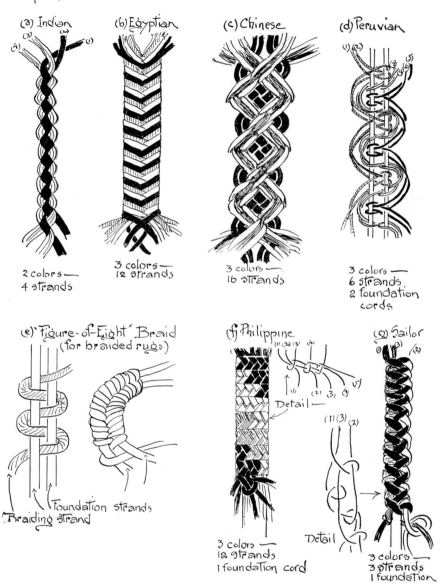

(a) Indian

2 colors —
4 strands

(b) Egyptian

3 colors —
12 strands

(c) Chinese

3 colors —
16 strands

(d) Peruvian

3 colors —
6 strands,
2 foundation
cords

(e) "Figure-of-Eight" Braid
(for braided rugs)

Foundation strands
Braiding strand

(f) Philippine

Detail —

3 colors —
12 strands
1 foundation cord

(g) Sailor

Detail

3 colors —
3 strands
1 foundation

Diagram No. 19

hand strand back to the left. This sounds more complicated than it is in practice.

As for most braids, it is well to attach a cord to the end and fasten it to a support of some kind, so that one may draw each tuck of the braid close. And in discontinuing the work it is well to make a loop tie with the strands of either side to hold the work in place so that it may be resumed without difficulty.

The braid sketched at (*b*) on the diagram is an ancient Egyptian braid, taken from the fringes that finish the ends of a piece of weaving in the Liverpool Museum in England. The piece is known as the "Girdle of Rameses" and there has been a good deal of discussion about it. Some experts insist that it may have been part of the ornamental trappings of Rameses' elephant, though hardly worn by the monarch himself. It is in linen, with an odd key-shaped pattern in the borders. At one time it was supposed to be an example of card-weaving, but as it does not show the twisted structure of a card-woven fabric this is clearly not the case.

The fringes are made of more strands than the one sketched, which, for the sake of clearness, shows only three colors—four strands of each. Any number of colors may be used but there must always be four strands of each color.

To begin the braid, arrange the strands so that there is a pair of each color on either side, the colors arranged in the same order. Suppose the order is with the two darkest strands first, then the two intermediate strands, and finally the two strands in the lightest color. Take one of the dark strands from the right-hand side across the remaining right-hand strands to the left. Take the other right-hand strand in the same color behind the other strands to the left. Then bring the first left-hand strand in the same color across in front to the right and the remaining dark strand on the left under the strands and across to the right. Continue in the same way with the four strands of each color. It will be noted that the pairs of strands come up side by side. It is the back strand that should be brought forward and the front strand that should be taken behind and across. Otherwise one may be surprised to discover that two separate braids are being produced instead of the single round braid desired.

This braid may be made over a foundation cord in the manner of a coxcomb if desired. For bag-handles and such things requiring length-wise strength, this is good practice.

In the fringes of the girdle of Rameses, the braids are tapered down to a point by suppressing certain strands in regular order.

An ancient Chinese braid is made with sixteen strands in three colors —eight strands of the lightest color and four strands each of the two other colors. The structure is simple and the braid is not difficult to make. Coarse material should be used and as for other braids the tucks should be drawn tight. This makes an attractive decorative edging for such things as lamp-shades.

The ancient Peruvian braid at (*d*) on the diagram has similar uses. It is made over two heavy foundation strands that should be stretched between two supports—the pegs of an inkle loom serve conveniently. The sketch is made in a very open manner for clearness. This braid should be made with coarse material in three colors as sketched and, like (*c*), may be used for a decorative binding.

The braid at (*e*) is by far the most practical braid for rugs, whether made of strips of rag or of coarse rug-yarns. As shown on the sketch, it is made with a single strand over a pair of foundation strands. The advantages of this braid lie in the firmness of the fabric produced—which may be as heavy as one chooses—and in the fact that the braids may be shaped with the greatest ease so that a flat rug results. The draw-back to most braided rugs is the difficulty of producing flatness.

Square rugs may be made as well as round and oval rugs. Also patterns may be produced in great variety. Mats made in raffia and similar material may also be made in this technique. In fact there are many practical uses and a whole craft may be based on it. Some sample pieces are shown on **Illustration No. 16.**

The foundation strands should be in balls and as long as convenient. The braiding strand may be in short lengths. If rags are used and fairly long strips are available, the material need not be sewed. Strips of rag should be folded lengthwise through the center, with the edges turned in to avoid loose threads, but if ironed they need not be sewed.

The sewing together of the braids should be done from time to time as the work progresses, and too long a braid should not be made before sewing, if the rug is to be shaped properly, and if a pattern is to be produced. The edges of the braids may be sewed together, but a firmer

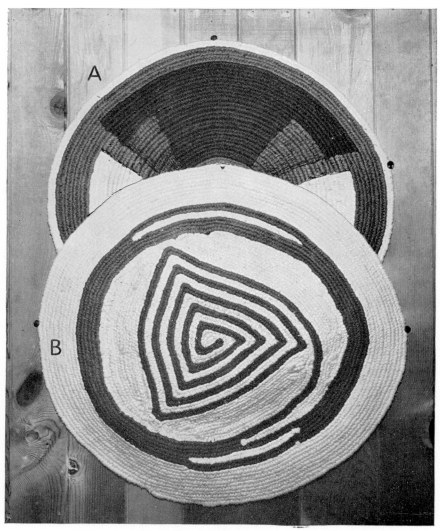

Illustration No. 16
Rugs in Figure-of-Eight braid, (*e*) Diagram 19

rug is produced by using a very long needle and sewing through two turns of the braid.

A "coxcomb" is a braid made over a foundation. For bag-handles, draw-cords and the like, this is a useful form of braid. The sketches at (*f*) and (*g*) show two coxcombs, and, as noted above, the Egyptian braid at (*b*) may also be used for the purpose.

The braid shown at (*f*) was evolved from the Philippine fringe-tie, given in the "Shuttle-craft Book," revised edition, at (*f*), **Diagram 72,** page 332. This braid makes a useful bag-handle, as the pattern material of the bag involved may be used in making it. A fairly heavy foundation cord should be used and the braiding strands may be comparatively fine. To make it, attach to the foundation cord the number of strands required to cover the foundation cord. These strands should be in groups of four ends of each color. The sketch shows four colors.

To braid, bring two strands from the left toward the right and make a half hitch around them with the third strand as indicated on the detail sketch. Drop the first thread and make a half hitch over strands 2 and 3 with the fourth strand. Continue in this manner, drawing each tuck of the braid close as you go. This braid takes some time to make, if the strands are fine—and it is not suitable for coarse material.

For a coxcomb in coarse material that may be made very rapidly, the one at (*g*) is practical and attractive. It is also made in half hitches as shown on the detail, but these are taken downward instead of upward as in the preceding coxcomb.

The Encyclopedia, referred to above, gives a large number of coxcombs and "cacklings," many of which will be found useful, though they are not all well adapted to the use of colored material, and for most of these macramé cord or a seine-twine should be used.

Diagram No. 20 shows some of the types of braiding used for belt-making, sometimes called "finger weaving." This seems to me a rather silly term, as of course all hand weaving is done with the fingers, and it is sometimes used loosely for other techniques, so it seems more reasonable simply to call it "braiding."

The belt-braid shown at (*a*) and (*b*) on **Diagram No. 20** is an ancient Peruvian braid. I prefer cotton as a material for this braid. The strand cottons—mercerized or unmercerized—are perhaps the best for the purpose. Very fine or very coarse materials are unsuitable. The warp ma-

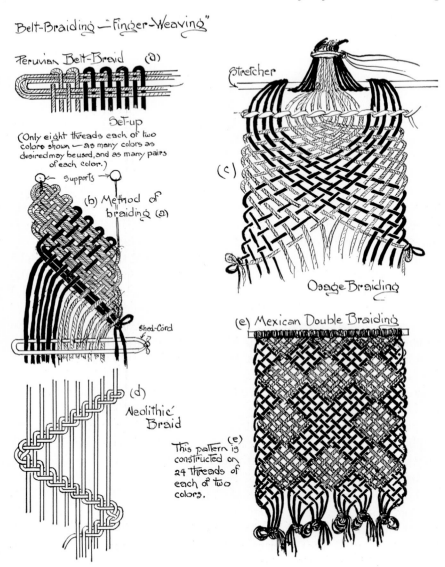

Belt-Braiding — "Finger-Weaving"

Peruvian Belt-Braid   (a)

Set-up

(Only eight threads each of two
colors shown — as many colors as
desired may be used, and as many pairs
of each color.)

⊙← Supports →
(b) Method of
braiding (a)

Shed-Cord

Stretcher

(c)

Osage Braiding

(e) Mexican Double Braiding

(d)
Neolithic
Braid

This pattern is
constructed on
24 threads of
each of two
colors.

(e)

Diagram No. 20

terial should be measured and cut in lengths twice the desired length of braid plus an allowance for take-up and for fringes if fringed ends are desired. There may be as many colors as one chooses and as many ends of each color as one desires.

The manner of setting up the braid is shown at (a) and the manner of braiding is shown at (b). In the sketch at (b), the braid is shown in open form for the sake of clearness but in making the braid, the threads slanted from right to left in single strands should be pushed close together to cover the double strands from left to right.

The method of braiding is to pick up a shed over the last double strand, working from right to left. Through this shed draw a pair of threads from the left to the right. Pick up a second shed in the same manner and draw through another pair of threads from the left. End by picking up a shed, which holds the last pair of threads—which may be considered the weft pair—in place. At this point I make a loop knot of these two weft strands at the right-hand edge to complete the set-up.

I do not know, of course, just how the ancient Peruvians went about making this braid, but the method I have found simplest and easiest is as follows: After attaching the braid to a support of some kind by a cord through the loop left at the beginning, I untie the loop-knot and wind the ends around a finger on the right hand. I then draw through the shed a new pair from the left-hand side, and make the pick-up of a new shed with the left hand, beginning at the left. I draw two more threads from the left through the new shed and again make the pick-up. After I have drawn through four pairs in this way I braid down the ends at the right, singly, over the other pairs, leaving two pairs in which I make the loop-knot while I draw up the threads and adjust the tension.

The work of the pick-up may be cut in half by tying a cord loosely through one or the other of the sheds as shown on the sketch. One of the sheds may then be made by drawing up this cord. This cord must be retied after each set of threads is braided down at the right in order to take in the new threads, so a loop-knot should be used in making the tie.

The sketch shows the braid in open form for the sake of clearness, but the threads should be drawn close together in the braiding to make a solid rep fabric.

This braid in finished form is shown on **Illustration No. 17.**

At (c) on **Diagram No. 20** is shown the set-up and method of braiding for the Osage braided girdles. The technique is in some ways similar to (*b*), though the effect is entirely different. The warp for this should be made on a warping board, though it is unnecessary to put in a cross or "lease." Only two colors are shown on the sketch, but as many colors may be introduced as desired. Usually three colors are used, 22 ends of each, arranged with 22 ends of one of the colors at the center and 11 ends of each of the other colors on either side of the center. On the diagram only two colors are indicated, with 10 ends of each.

The best material for girdles in this braid is a heavy knitting worsted, and the colors used should be bright and in strong contrast. These girdles are very effective when worn over a simple dress in plain color.

The warp should be made over the bars of a warping board or over supports that permit laying it out flat as it will be woven. The length should be about two yards, to allow for take-up and the long fringes.

The braiding may be done beginning at one end, above the fringes, but it is more convenient to begin at the center. If to be made in this manner a row of twining should be made across the warp at the center, before the warp is released from the warping board. The twining should be made with a double end of one of the colors, each tucked around two warp-ends, and should be drawn tight.

After the warp is taken from the board, a stretcher should be inserted close to the twining, as shown at (*c*), **Diagram No. 20.** This may be a small stick or a heavy knitting needle. The warp should then be cut at each end, and the part of the warp above the stretcher should be chained to keep it in order. A cord should then be tied tight around the warp between the stretcher and the chain, and the warp may then be hung by this cord to a support of some kind. This completes the set-up.

To begin the braiding, cross the two threads at the center, and carry the thread from the left of the center over and under toward the right, and pick up the opposite shed, working from right to left. Turn the braid over and do the same with the other thread at the center, braiding again from left to right and picking up a shed. Take a second thread from the left of the center toward the right through the picked-up shed, and pick up the shed again. Make a loop tie in the two threads so drawn through. Turn the braid over and again braid two threads from left to right, picking up the shed after each cross thread, and make a loop tie. After two more threads have been braided across on each side, braid down the

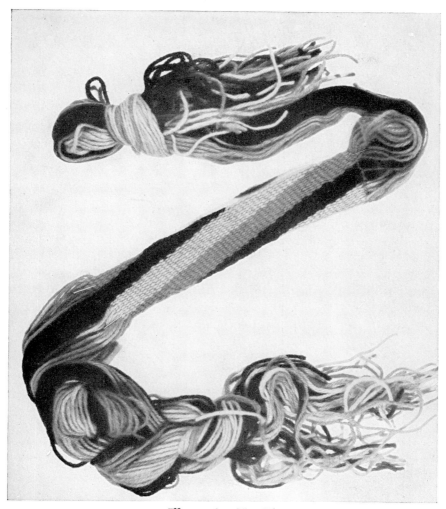

Illustration No. 17

Belt in Peruvian belt-braiding

upper pair of threads over the second pair, on each side. Continue in this manner. A reference to the sketch at (c), **Diagram 20,** will make the process clear. On the sketch the threads are shown separated, for the sake of clearness, but the cross-threads should be pushed close together to make a firm fabric, as shown on **Illustration 18.**

Illustration No. 18

Girdle in Osage braiding, braided both ways from the center and finished
with long braided fringes

When the first half of the braid is complete, finish off the fringes in the
four-strand Indian braid shown at (*a*), **Diagram 19.**

When the first half of the girdle is complete, release the chained part
of the warp, attach the finished end to the support, and beginning again
at the twining, make the second half of the piece. The row of twining
may be taken out or left in as preferred. There will be a diamond figure
at the center, followed by a succession of chevrons.

It is customary to make these girdles the exact length to fit the waist, the girdle being secured by tying together groups of the fringe braids.

A similar form of braiding is produced in Sweden, but instead of braiding from the center outward toward the edges, the Swedish weavers braid from the edges toward the center. This method produces U-figures instead of chevrons.

Illustration No. 19

Various styles of Osage braiding

There are many variations of this simple—but not too easy—technique, a few of which are shown on **Illustration 19.** An elaborate form of this braiding was widely practiced in Canada in the early days for the making of wide sashes worn by the "coureurs des bois." These were made in fine, hard-twisted wool yarns. **Illustration 21** shows a part of one of these ancient pieces. The craft is being revived in Canada and an interesting pamphlet is available, "The Assomption Sash," by Marius Barbeau, Bulletin 93, Anthropological Series 24, National Museum of Canada.

The wide sashes are extremely handsome but the beginner is advised to become thoroughly familiar with the simple Osage braiding be-

Illustration No. 20

Mexican double braiding

fore setting up a "ceinture flèché," as this is not a project for a novice.

The braid at (*d*), **Diagram No. 20,** is extremely ancient. I have reproduced it from a photograph in the *Ciba Review* of a piece of weaving dating from the Neolithic period. Done in heavy silk or gold cord, this makes a handsome evening girdle. It looks as though it might not be very substantial, and as though the meshes might tend to slide together, but this is not the case, as experiment will show. This is not, of course, a braid for fine material. As the manner of braiding is clearly shown on the diagram it need not be described here.

The double braiding shown at (*e*), **Diagram No. 20** may be used for belts and decorative bands of all kinds. In Mexico the technique is often used for the upper edge finish of bags done in the double-plain weave, the figures being braided down to points and the ends knotted, with a draw-cord put through the mesh under the cords. In ancient Peru, bags and other pieces were made in this fashion—some in extremely intricate patterns. There were even some triple braids done in three colors.

The method is clearly shown on the diagram. For a simple pattern of diamond figures as shown on the diagram and in **Illustration 20,** braid the light-colored part of the warp, over and under, into a series of points. Loop the threads together in groups. Turn the braid over, and braid the dark color into points in the same manner. Then, with the dark part of the warp still on top, change the threads from front to back and

Illustration No. 21

Detail of an ancient *Ceinture Flèché,* braiding similar to Osage braiding. Type of girdle worn by the *Coureurs des Bois* in old-time Canada

back to front, a figure at a time. Braid down the light-colored threads and loop together. Turn the braid over and braid the corresponding figure in the dark threads on the other side. And so continue.

The sketch shows the braid in an open mesh for the sake of clearness, but it should be drawn close to make a true double-plain fabric.

PART V

Plaiting

PLAITING IS AN EXTREMELY ANCIENT FORM of weaving and of very wide distribution. Egyptian pieces dating back to 2,000 B.C. have been discovered and a plaited hair-net attributed to the Bronze Age has been found in Denmark. There are also very ancient Peruvian examples. The beaded and jeweled hair-nets worn by the ladies in medieval times in Europe were made in this manner. And today the Indian women of Guiana plait the slings in which they carry their babies on their backs, and Hopi Indian bridegrooms plait the white wedding girdles for their prospective brides. In Mexico large bags of fiber and handsome hammocks are made in plaiting.

In the Scandinavian countries, plaiting has been revived where it is called "sprangning" and is used chiefly in the form of coarse lace for borders and fringes. It is said to be the most ancient form of lacemaking known, and has somewhat the form of simple bobbin lace.

Only the simple "native" forms of the craft will be presented here. Those who are interested in "sprangning" will find notes on the subject and many excellent illustrations in "Swedish Textiles," edited by Emelie Walterstorff; and information on the ancient Egyptian forms of the craft will be found in "Egyptisch Vlechtwerk" by E. S. Van Reesema—unfortunately in the Dutch language, but entirely usable because of the excellent diagrams and illustrations.

EQUIPMENT. No equipment is required except a support of some kind for the work and a number of small sticks of suitable length. Narrow pieces may be set up conveniently over the pegs of an inkle loom—the heddle-peg and stretcher peg being removed. For wide pieces, a frame of some sort is required.

70

The sticks may be round or flat, specially-made slips of hard wood, or wooden or plastic knitting needles. Metal knitting needles or wires are not desirable as they tend to fall out of the work, with disconcerting results. For hammocks and large shopping bags in jute or twine, fairly heavy sticks are required, but for wool scarves, silk neckties and similar projects, small sticks or fine knitting needles are better. The minimum number is eight, and it is often convenient to have more.

The warp—which is also the weft, as in braiding—does not hang free, but should be anchored at both ends. A continuous warp is best for most purposes. If a frame is used, the material should be carried around a stout bar at top and bottom, and one of the bars should be removable to permit adjustment of the tension to allow for take-up.

The material may be what one pleases, and colors as varied as one likes. No elaborate patterns are possible in the simple forms of plaiting described here, but various effects of stripes and diagonals in color may be produced, as shown on the illustration.

An amusing feature of plaiting is that one weaves at both ends at the same time. Where the two fabrics come together at the center, a few shots of tabby must be inserted to hold the weave. The quality of the fabric is its elasticity—greater in some of the weaves than in others. Several forms of plaiting may be combined in one piece with interesting results.

SET–UP. The set-up for plaiting is the same for all forms. It consists simply in winding the material regularly and evenly between the upper and lower supports of a frame or the front and back pegs of an inkle loom. For a continuous warp the ends should not be tied to the pegs, but should be tied to each other around the end peg, as in making a set-up for inkle-weaving.

WEAVING TECHNIQUE. It is well to begin a piece of plaiting by inserting several tabby weft shots as indicated on the diagram. These may be few or many as preferred. Open the shed for the first tabby shot and insert a weft at each end of the stretched band. Open the opposite shed and bring the weft shots back. Repeat as desired. After making the last tabby shot, put a stick through the shed at either end.

For the weave at (*a*), **Diagram No. 21,** cross thread 2 to the right over

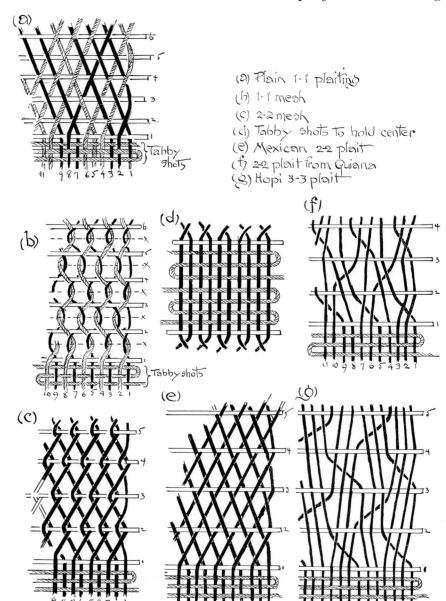

(a) Plain 1-1 plaiting
(b) 1-1 mesh
(c) 2-2 mesh
(d) Tabby shots to hold center
(e) Mexican 2-2 plait
(f) 2-2 plait from Guiana
(g) Hopi 3-3 plait

Diagram No. 21

thread 1, and pick up thread 1. In the same manner, cross thread 4 over thread 3 and pick up 3. Proceed in the same manner all across, and insert a stick under the picked-up shed. Push it down against the tabby heading. Put a second stick through the same shed and push it back against the other tabby heading.

For the next shed, cross thread 1 over thread 4 and pick up 4; cross 3 over 6 and pick up 6, and so all across. Insert a second pair of sticks. Proceed in the same manner, crossing the threads first from left to right and then from right to left. After four pairs of sticks have been inserted, on the fifth shed, withdraw the first sticks and put them in again through the new shed, both at top and bottom of the weaving.

In picking up the sheds, insert the fingers of the left hand through the shed along with the last stick and make the pick-up from right to left with the right hand.

When finally the sticks come so close together at the center that no further pick-up is possible, take out the sticks one by one, till only the last pair remains in the work. Through this shed, take a tape-needle carrying a double end of material like the warp. Separate the two strands, pressing them against the edges of the weaving, and take out the last two sticks. Pick up a tabby shed on the needle and again separate the two strands. Continue till the space is filled, and put in a final single strand at the center, as indicated at (*d*) on the diagram.

For a plaited bag, these tabby shots will make the bottom of the bag, and should be put in quite firmly. For a scarf or necktie they may be left fairly loose or drawn tight as preferred.

At (*b*) on the diagram is shown the method of making a 1–1 mesh. Begin with the first right-hand thread under stick No. 1, take thread No. 2 over and under thread 1, picking up thread No. 2. Make the same twist with each pair of threads all across and put in a pair of sticks. For the next shed, do nothing with thread No. 1, but take thread 3 under and over thread No. 2. Pick up thread 2. Make the same twist with each pair all across and put in a pair of sticks. And so continue. Some people find it easier to put in additional sticks where the dotted lines marked "X" are shown on the diagram, but the other system is more rapid. If a long mesh is desired, as for a draw-string, each pair of threads may be given two or more twists instead of the single twist sketched.

The 2–2 mesh shown at (*c*) is an extremely elastic fabric and is the weave most used for neckties. It is also good for the upper part of bags. For most purposes it is better than the weave at (*b*) and is also somewhat easier to make, as the crossings are all in the same direction.

Begin with thread 1 over the first stick. Cross thread 3 over threads 1 and 2 and pick up 1. Cross thread 5 over threads 4 and 2 and pick up 2. And so all across. For the second shed, cross thread 1 over thread 3. Cross thread 2 over threads 5 and 3 and pick up 3. Cross thread 4 over 7 and 5 and pick up 5, and so all across. Check from time to time to make sure of crossing over two threads each time. The third pick-up is like the first and the fourth is like the second.

At (*e*) is shown the Mexican plain 2–2 plait which is probably used more than any other form of plaiting. For some reason that I have never been able to understand, people have more difficulty with this plait than with any other. The trouble appears to be in doing the edges correctly. The following procedure may simplify the problem. Begin with the odd-numbered threads over stick No. 1, as shown on the diagram. Draw the first three odd-numbered threads toward the right. This will bring thread No. 5 across thread No. 2. Pick up 2. To correct the edge, take thread No. 1 back into the weave by carrying it under thread 3 and picking it up. Continue across: thread 7 across 6 and 4, pick up 4, and so all across. When the left-hand edge is reached, there will be three threads together, either over or under the stick depending on the number of threads in the set-up. Correct the edge by turning back the last thread and bringing it between the other two in the group of three.

For the following shed, the first thread on the right—thread No. 3— will be under the stick. Draw out to the right the first three threads under the stick—threads 3, 5 and 7. Pick up thread 7. Correct the edge by taking thread 3 across thread 5 and picking up 5. If it is kept in mind that the free thread on the edge must turn back into the weave, and that the regular alternation of over and under must be preserved, the thing should cause no trouble, though it may seem confusing at first.

The Mexican set-up is usually made in red, white and blue, as follows: three threads blue; (*) twelve threads white; six threads red; 12 threads white; six threads blue; repeat from (*) as desired for width. End with 12 threads white and 6 threads red; 12 threads white; 3 threads blue. Of course other colors may be used in a similar arrangement of three colors. The scarf shown on **Illustration No. 22** is in this plait.

The plait from Guiana, at (*f*) on the diagram, looks intricate, but is easier to produce than might appear. It is shown in very open form on the drawing for the sake of clearness, but should be woven close, making a quite solid fabric useful for belts and girdles. The effect is of lengthwise twilled ribs with diagonal or diamond effects of color if the warp is made in stripes of color.

This is a 2–2 plait and the material should be set up with an odd number of ends—in pairs with an extra, as shown on the diagram. This extra thread should be under stick No. 1 when the work begins, as sketched. Slant threads 2 and 3 across to the right and pick up thread 1. Pick up thread 4. Slant 7 and 6 across 5 and pick up 5 and 8. Continue in this manner all across and put in the sticks.

For the next shed there will be two threads on the right-hand edge under the stick—threads 2 and 3. Pick up 3. Slant threads 1 and 4 to the left and pick up 6. Pick up 7, and continue in this manner all across. Put in the sticks.

The third pick-up will be like the first, and the fourth will be like the second. The rhythm, when acquired, is easy to follow, but care must be taken to keep the threads in correct order. Keep in mind that at the beginning of each pick-up there will be alternately one thread under the stick or two threads under the stick, and that after the first pick-up there will be two threads over and two under all the way across.

At (*g*) on the diagram is a similar plait done in threes instead of in pairs. This is the plait used by the Hopi Indians for their ceremonial white wedding sashes. As made by the Hopis, these sashes are done in fine white cotton with as many as 150 ends.

The Hopi manner of making the plait is somewhat different from the method described for (*f*), above. But as it seems a good deal more difficult I shall not describe it. Anyone who is interested will find it given in detail in a pamphlet, "Pueblo Crafts" by Underhill, printed at the Haskell Institute Print Shop, Lawrence, Kansas.

The fabric produced is similar to (*f*), differing only in that it is heavier. In making the set-up, use a number of ends divisible by three, with one thread in addition. The manner of picking up the sheds is clearly shown on the diagram and should give no trouble. There is, however, a greater chance of taking up the threads in incorrect order in this plait than in (*f*), and such an error is disfiguring. As it is sometimes

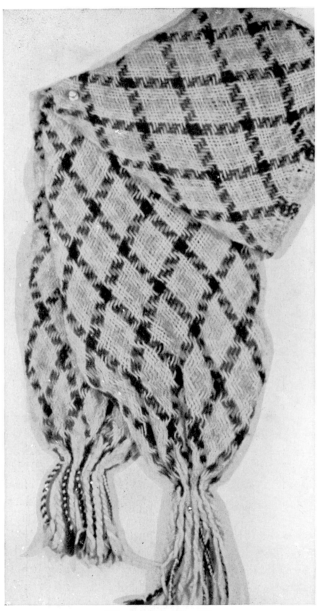

Illustration No. 22
Scarf in three colors, Mexican 2–2 plaiting, (*e*) Diagram 21

quite difficult to go back more than two spaces to correct an error, I find it good practice to use more sticks. The number at the working end may be kept to four, but additional sticks may be permitted to accumulate at the upper end of the weaving.

The forms of plaiting at (*e*), (*f*) and (*g*) are the most satisfactory for belts and wide girdles; also for scarves and bags. In Mexico, plait (*e*) is extensively used for large bags and for hammocks, done in sisal or jute. The same plait in soft cottons is used for girdles and scarves. Plait (*c*) also makes an excellent hammock. I saw one in Mexico made in two colors, alternately light and dark, with the light threads apparently stretched tight and the dark threads allowed to lie loose. In making the set-up for this plait, the dark threads should be at least twice as long as the light threads.

As far as I know, plaiting has not been extensively used in the hospital practice of occupational therapy. It might, I believe, prove a useful craft for this purpose, as the equipment is so simple, and the set-up might be attached so easily to a hospital bed. Also it appeals to those who prefer a fairly large project such as a bag or scarf to the weaving of narrow bands.

PART VI

—— *A Group of Belt-Weaves* ——

1: A PERUVIAN TWO–WARP WEAVE

THE BELT-MAKING TECHNIQUE described below is probably one of the most ancient forms of decorative weaving extant. Most of the examples come from Peru, where the technique is still used.

The fabric produced has structural drawbacks, though these may be minimized by careful designing. The technique is, however, simple and easy and lends itself to amusing patterns, very free in form, and the effect is sprightly in the extreme.

In Mexico the same technique is fairly common, but is used for wide pieces such as runners, rather than for belts.

Three sheds are required, and in Peru the primitive belt loom is used, but modern American weavers find this form of loom inconvenient. The inkle loom may be used if a small hole-and-slot heddle—to carry the pattern threads—is added, in front of the heddles. But a harness loom is desirable.

This is a weave for fairly coarse material, and two separate warps are involved. The foundation warp, set close enough to cover the weft, may however be of fine cotton either threaded double: 1,1,2,2,1,1,2,2, and so on or: 1,1,1, 2,2,2, and so on. The pattern material should be a coarse wool, a coarse strand cotton, or something similar. The weft material should be like the foundation warp, but coarser.

Because of the structure of the fabric the take-up of the foundation warp is greater than the take-up of the pattern threads so that the pattern threads become slack as weaving progresses. If the loom used is equipped with two warp-beams, the two warps may be wound separately, but as few small looms are provided with two beams, this difficulty may

78

be overcome as sketched at (*a*), **Diagram No. 22.** As soon as the slack becomes troublesome, raise the pattern warp by treadling on 5 and insert a stick under the raised threads, behind the heddles. Carry the stick over the back-beam and down to a position under the warp-beam and attach it to the bottom beam of the loom by means of cords and snitch-knots, as shown on the diagram. By adjusting the knots from time to time as becomes necessary, the slack may be taken up.

Only three sheds are required for this weave and all the pattern threads may be threaded on harness 3 with the foundation threads on harnesses 1 and 2. However it is more convenient to thread the pattern threads on harnesses 3 and 4 as shown on the draft—or in groups of three or four threads on each harness—and small pattern effects may be woven without a pick-up. For free figures, however, the pick-up stick is used. The figures illustrated on **Diagram No. 22** contemplate a pattern warp of 37 warp-ends. These are typical Peruvian patterns adapted from various ancient pieces.

The Mexican manner of using the weave is described in my "Shuttle-Craft Book," the revised edition, Chapter Nineteen beginning on page 293. These directions will not be repeated here.

Weavers will enjoy designing patterns of their own. Extreme freedom of design is possible. The only caution is that the designer should keep in mind the fact that when the pattern threads do not appear on the surface they are making skips on the reverse side, and that unless the piece is to be lined, it is important to tie these long floats into the fabric from time to time, as shown by the apparently meaningless dashes, dots and small figures in the background of some of the patterns illustrated. In a closely designed figure such as (*e-6*) on the diagram, the dots and dashes are unnecessary.

The method of weaving is extremely simple. Treadle 1 and 2 alternately throughout for the foundation fabric, with the pattern pick-up on treadle 5, as shown on the tie-ups given on the diagram. Treadles 3 and 4 may be omitted from the tie-up, but, if included, may be used to make a pattern of small squares.

For the narrow solid lines all across, treadle on 5, which raises all the pattern threads, and put a stick through the shed. With the stick in place, treadle 1 and weave, treadle 2 and weave—in a weft the color of the foundation warp and somewhat coarser. For plain background all

Two-Warp Belt-Weave —Peruvian

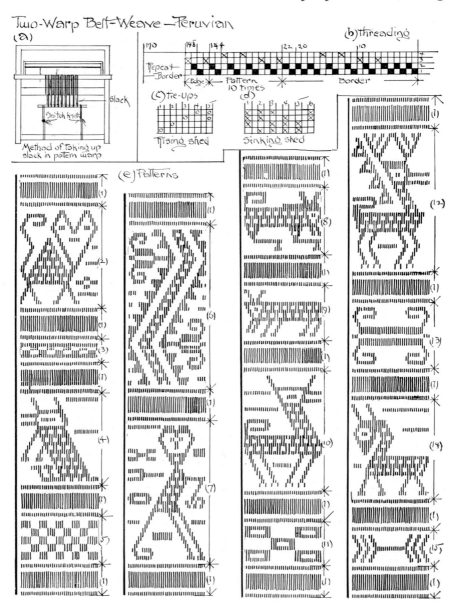

Diagram No. 22

across, treadle and weave 1 and 2 as may be required. For broad bands in pattern warp, treadle 5 and insert the stick, treadle and weave 1,2, repeated as may be desired. In weaving, use a flat "poke-shuttle" wider than the stick and beat against the shuttle in the shed. To produce a figure, treadle 5 and take up on the pick-up stick the threads required for the figure in question. Treadle 1 and weave; treadle 2 and weave.

Sometimes threads not desired in the pattern may appear in the background, especially if the pattern warp has become slack. To control this, after making the pick-up for the pattern, treadle 1–2 if tie-up (*c*) is used or treadle 6, on tie-up (*d*). Insert a stick over the depressed pattern threads and under the raised threads. Then weave the two foundation shots on 1 and on 2 as usual.

Though, as noted above, this weave does not produce a very sound fabric, because of the fact that the pattern warp does not interweave firmly with the ground, simply passing over and under the ground—sometimes in fairly long skips—it is highly decorative and may be used for a number of purposes. If used as a belt or girdle, however, it should be lined with a firm fabric. This may be woven at the same time as the decorated part of the piece by making the foundation warp wide enough to turn under. This extra width of the foundation fabric may be all on one side or the other of the pattern strip, or half on each side.

2: A DOUBLE–FACED WEAVE

One of the handsomest and most interesting of the "native" belt-weaves is a double-faced, warp-faced weave used widely in Peru, in the wild Gran Chaco district of South America, in Bolivia, and sometimes seen in Mexico. Oddly enough, it appears to be unknown in Guatemala.

The product of this weave is a very firm four-ply fabric with the same pattern on both sides—with the colors reversed.

In Peru the warp is usually set in stripes using four colors—two colors, a light and a dark, for a stripe on either side of a central stripe in two additional colors, also a light and a dark color. The middle stripe is usually half as wide as the side stripes. Sometimes there are more than three stripes, half the warp being white or in a light color with narrow stripes in two or more colors for the other half of the warp. This arrangement produces figures in white on a striped ground on one side of the piece and figures in stripes against a white ground on the reverse.

In the Peruvian and Bolivian pieces, many intricate patterns may be found, though the one sketched on **Diagram No. 23** is the one seen most frequently. The figures are woven in 1,2,3,4, order throughout, with the help of the pick-up stick. Why the humanesque figures have neither nose nor mouth I do not know, but this appears to be the manner in which they are always woven. Perhaps there is some ancient tradition to account for this lack of the usual features, as it would be a simple matter to introduce them if one were so minded. As it is, the effect is quite modernistic, as is so much of ancient Peruvian design.

The Gran Chaco pieces are done in red and white or black and white, sometimes in red, black and white, always in bold geometric figures, a few of which are shown on **Diagram No. 24.** The effect is extremely striking. Sometimes in the Gran Chaco, ponchos are woven in this technique, but they are so thick and heavy that they appear clumsy.

EQUIPMENT.   Four sheds are required for this weave and though the native pieces are woven on the primitive type of body loom with shed sticks, a small four-harness loom is, for most of us, more convenient.

MATERIAL.   All the pieces in this weave that I have had the pleasure of examining have been done in a hard-twisted wool of medium weight. This is a material not readily found on our market, unfortunately. I have experimented with cottons and other materials but have found nothing else that gives as good an effect, though the coarse cottons—#5 or #3 perle cottons, for instance, or even a good grade of carpet warp—may be used with fairly satisfactory results. A soft worsted yarn will not serve at all, but of course those whose equipment includes a spinning wheel may re-spin such yarns to the desired texture.

The warp should be set close enough to cover the weft completely. If wool is used for the warp it is wise to dispense with the reed. The weft may be a coarse cotton.

WEAVING.   This weave may be produced in two different ways. I prefer method two, as described below, as it has the smoother rhythm, but many weavers find method one the simpler. Which is preferred by the

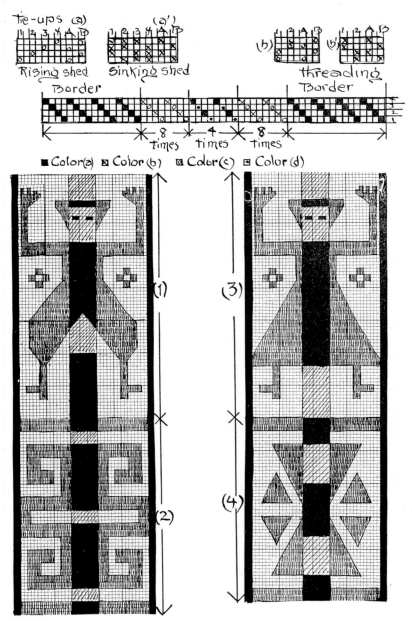

Diagram No. 23

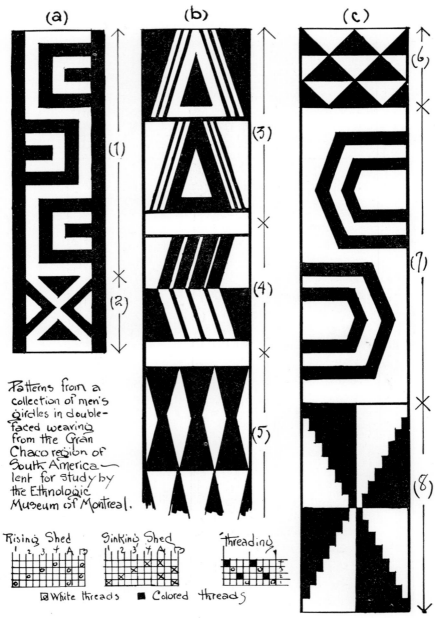

(a)   (b)   (c)

(1) (2) (3) (4) (5) (6) (7) (8)

Patterns from a
collection of men's
girdles in double-
faced weaving
from the Gran
Chaco region of
South America—
lent for study by
the Ethnologic
Museum of Montreal.

Rising Shed   Sinking Shed   Threading

☑ White threads   ■ Colored threads

Diagram No. 24

84

"native" weavers I do not know as I have never seen this weave in production. Either weave may be used for any pattern.

For Method One, the tie-ups at (*b*) and (*b'*), **Diagram No. 23**, are the most convenient. Either method may be used on the tie-ups shown on **Diagram No. 24.**

For Method One, to weave all across in the lighter color or colors: treadle A and weave; treadle 1 and weave; treadle A and weave; treadle 2 and weave. Repeat as desired. To weave the dark color all across, treadle and weave: B,1,B,2, and repeat.

To produce a figure, treadle B and take up on a small pick-up stick all the dark threads desired for the figure. Treadle A and take up on a second stick all the light threads of the background. Insert a shed-stick under the raised threads; set the shed-stick on edge and weave. If, in making the second pick-up, a stick is used wide enough to serve as a shed-stick and this is taken under the raised threads of the first pick-up as well as under the desired light threads, it may be set on edge for the passage of the shuttle. Take out the stick, treadle 1 and weave. Make the same pick-up as before and weave. Take out the stick; treadle 2 and weave.

This is the complete process. It will be noted that the pick-up is made on alternate sheds only, the intervening sheds being woven plain.

For Method Two, use the tie-ups at (*a*) and (*a'*) **Diagram No. 30** —or the tie-ups as given on **Diagram 24** if one prefers. For plain light on top, treadle 1 and insert a pick-up stick. Treadle 3 and weave. Leaving the stick in place treadle 2 and weave. Take out the stick. Treadle 3 and insert the stick; treadle 1 and weave; treadle 4 and weave. Repeat. For dark on top, treadle 2 and insert the stick; treadle 4 and weave; treadle 1 and weave. Take out the stick. Treadle 4 and insert the stick. Treadle 2 and weave; treadle 3 and weave. Repeat.

For the pattern, treadle 2 and insert a stick under the threads corresponding to the figure. Treadle 1 and take up the light threads of the background. Treadle 4 and weave. It will be noted that the dark threads mesh. Take out the stick under the dark pick-up and put it in again under the new dark shed, ahead of the stick under the light threads. Treadle 3 and weave. This time the light threads mesh. Take out the stick under the light pick-up and put it in again under the new light shed, ahead of the other stick. Treadle 2 and weave. And so continue.

This may sound complicated as set down in words but it is a simple rhythm in practice.

It will be noted that in Method Two, the A and B treadles are not used. They may be omitted from the tie-up if one chooses, as they are useful only in weaving headings.

This is, in my opinion, one of the handsomest of the South American belt-weaves. The technique may also be used for wide fabrics if one chooses. It produces a very firm, heavy fabric. The pattern possibilities are practically unlimited. The Gran Chaco patterns have a vigorous, barbaric feeling that is more effective than the perhaps more sophisticated feeling of the Peruvian style. This is, of course, a matter of taste. For a ski-belt or headband, nothing could be handsomer than a piece in this weave.

3: A GROUP OF SIMILAR WARP–FACED WEAVES

The weaves described below appear to be almost unknown among us. These weaves, to be sure, are not "kindergarten" types of weaving and are not recommended for first adventures into the textile arts, but will give a weaver of some experience an interesting and not too difficult bit of exercise. And when one thinks of the "primitive" people who devised and practice these weaves, one may come to realize that to be primitive is not to be mentally subnormal or inept.

These weaves are from ancient Peru and (in a somewhat varied form) Bolivia. One—oddly enough—is from Estonia.

These are all apparently very ancient weaves though they are still current practice, except perhaps one of the Peruvian weaves which I at least have never seen in a modern piece. The South American weaves were no doubt produced on the primitive "body loom" or on a warp staked out flat on the ground, as is the Bolivian native custom. They are the same on both sides of the fabric, with the colors reversed. The Estonian weave is not the same on both sides; it is somewhat easier to weave than the similar South American weaves. It is possible to weave the Estonian patterns in the South American manner, or to weave the South American patterns in the manner of Estonia. The set-up is the same.

Pattern of Estonian Bag

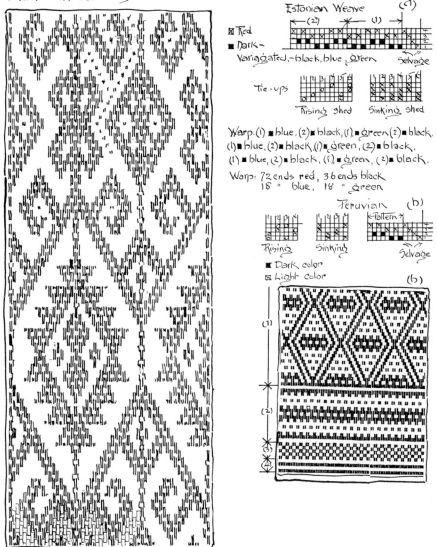

Estonian Weave (a)

⊠ Red
■ Dark-
Variagated,-black, blue, green

Tie-ups

Rising shed   Sinking shed

Warp: (1) ■ blue, (2) ■ black, (1), ■ green (2) ■ black,
(1) ■ blue, (2) ■ black, (1) ■ green, (2) ■ black,
(1) ■ blue, (2) ■ black, (1) ■ green, (2) ■ black.

Warp: 72 ends red, 36 ends black
      18 " blue, 18 " green

Peruvian (b)

Rising   Sinking   Pattern

Selvage

■ Dark color
⊠ Light color   (b)

Diagram No. 25

THE ESTONIAN WEAVE.   As the Estonian weave is the simpler of the
techniques, it will be presented first. The pattern shown on **Diagram
No. 25** is that of a bag, part of the weave of which is shown at (*a*). The
piece is in two strips sewed together down the center, and I have
been told that this weave is never attempted in a wide piece—though
I see no good reason why it should not be if one wished. The warp is in
four colors arranged as indicated on the draft, the red color being used
throughout for the background with the figure carried out in the striped
black, blue and green. The warp is a fine, hard-twisted cotton about a
20/2 in count, and the warp-setting is 80 ends to the inch. The weave
might, of course, be developed in coarser material and would make an
excellent fabric for chair-seats and the like, as it is extremely firm. I have
woven it in a 10/3 mercerized cotton at a setting of 48 ends to the inch.
The weft may be slightly coarser than the warp, but not too heavy.

The technique is a simple pick-up technique and progresses quite
rapidly. To weave the figure sketched, beginning at the bottom, treadle
on 2 and pick up a pair at the center of one of the figures. Skip one pair,
pick up one, skip two, pick up one, skip two, pick up three, skip two,
pick up one, skip two, pick up one, skip one and repeat. With the pick-up
stick in position, treadle 6 and weave. Treadle 3 and pick up the background. With the stick in position treadle 5 and weave. Treadle on 1
and make the second pattern pick-up; treadle 6 and weave. Treadle on 4
and make the corresponding background pick-up. Treadle 5 and weave.
This is the complete process.

For the sake of clearness, I have not attempted to show the background pick-ups on the drawing except for a short distance at the bottom of the drawing on the left. If, as in the Estonian piece, a black weft
is used, there will be small black dots as sketched at the top of the
drawing. If the weft is red, these dots will not appear. They are not warp
dots as in the Peruvian weave shown at (*b*) on **Diagram No. 26.**

SOME SOUTH AMERICAN WEAVES.   The four weaves described on
the following pages are practiced largely in Peru but are also known
elsewhere. They are of varying degrees of difficulty.

I. AN ANCIENT PERUVIAN WEAVE.   The weave at (*b*) on **Diagram No. 25** may be used for pieces as wide as desired, or for narrow

Three-Color Weaves

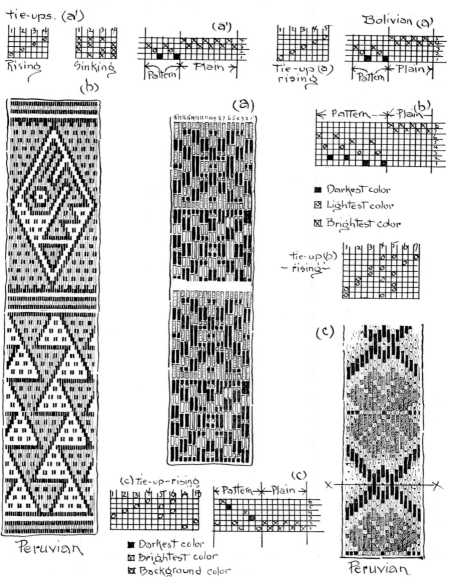

tie-ups. (a')

Rising   Sinking

(a')

Plain

Pattern ← → Plain

(b)

(a)

Bolivian (a)

Tie-up (a) rising

Pattern ← → Plain

← Pattern → ← Plain → (b)

■ Darkest color
☑ Lightest color
⊠ Brightest color

tie-up (b) – rising

(c)

Peruvian

(c) Tie-up-rising

(c)

← Pattern → ← Plain →

■ Darkest color
☑ Brightest color
⊠ Background color

Peruvian

Diagram No. 26

Illustration No. 23

South American belt weaves. On the left, typical Peruvian pattern; on the right, Gran Chaco patterns

90

strips of pattern between areas of plain rep as frequently seen in South American weavings, used especially for bags. It will be noted that the manner of threading is exactly the same as for the Estonian weave at (*a*) above, but the tie-up is different. If used with a plain rep, however, six harnesses should be used, the two additional harnesses for the plain

Illustration No. 24

South American weaves. Left to right: Bolivian; Bolivian, draft (*a*) Diagram 26; Peruvian, draft (*b*) Diagram 25

weave. It is true that a plain weave might be picked up on a twill threading, as given for a selvage, but this would be somewhat complicated and is not recommended.

The pattern sketched might be woven in the manner of the Estonian weave, but if woven as noted below will produce the same pattern on both sides of the fabric, with the colors reversed. This may or may not be important. For bags, chair-seats and such pieces the wrong side of the fabric is not in evidence, but for such things as table mats a reversible weave is desirable.

For the plain cross-bars as sketched at the bottom of the design—section (4)—weave treadles 1,2,1,2 and repeat as desired. For section (3), weave treadles 3,4,3,4 and repeat as desired. For section (2), weave as follows: treadles 2,1,3,2,4,2,3,1,4,1,3,2,4,2,3,1,2. Section (1) requires a pick-up, as follows: treadle 1, treadle 3, treadle 1 and make the pick-up as shown on the sketch, taking up four threads at the point of the diamond, skip two, take up 16, skip 2, take up 2, skip 2 and repeat. Treadle 2 and take up the light pairs between the picked-up dark threads. Weave. Treadle 4 and weave. Treadle 1 and make the second dark pick-up. Treadle 2 and make the light pick-up. Weave. Treadle 3 and weave. Continue in this manner all the way, weaving plain on 3 and 4 and making pick-ups as required by the pattern on 1 and 2.

This is somewhat more difficult than the Estonian weave, as noted above, but is not complicated when one acquires the rhythm. The Estonian pattern might be woven in the same manner and would then weave the design in red against a striped black, blue and green background on the reverse side of the fabric.

A Bolivian bag in my possession was woven in the Peruvian manner, in fine material and in a variety of figures which in the piece are in white against a ground in stripes of color, black, green, maroon and two shades of red, the pattern stripes being separated by stripes in plain rep.

II. A BOLIVIAN WEAVE. Oddly enough, the little weave shown at (*a*), **Diagram No. 26,** seems to be the most difficult to produce among this group of special weaves. However it is not too troublesome after one acquires the way of it, and it makes a handsome belt as can be surmised from the diagram. The set-up, as will be noted, requires five harnesses, harnesses 4 and 5 being used for the plain rep borders. It is possible to produce the rep by threading these borders: 3,4,3,4 and repeat, and using the pick-up stick for one of the sheds, but this is troublesome and somewhat confusing and, if possible, five harnesses should be used.

The pattern, as illustrated, requires 18 warp-ends in each of three colors, and to be effective, coarse material should be used. The piece shown on the illustration was made in a coarse knitting worsted, and the colors used were black, yellow, and a strong blue-green. The blue-green—(x) on the diagram—was the color used in both figures. One figure is green and black, with the reverse side in green and yellow.

Then the second figure is green and yellow on top and green and black on the reverse.

The weaving goes like this: Weave the solid stripes 3–4, 1–2–5 and repeat, ending on 1–2–4. Treadle 1 and make the first pick-up—under two, over four, under two, over two, under two, over four, under two. Treadle 3 and make the opposite pick-up—over two, under four, over two, under two, over two, under four, over two. Treadle 5 and weave. For the second shot, treadle 1 and make the first pick-up—under two threads, over four, under two, over two, under two, over four, under two. Let treadle 1 go, and treadle 3, make the opposite pick-up—over two, under four, over two, under two, over two, under four, over two. Let treadle 3 go. Treadle 4 and weave.

For the second pick-up, treadle 3—over four, pick up two, over six, pick up two, over four. Treadle 2 and make the opposite pick-up. This seems confusing as it brings up the yellow threads, not seen on top. This pick-up is for the figure on the under side. Treadle 1–5 and weave. Continue in this manner till the figure is complete. End by treadling and weaving 1–2–6.

For the second figure treadle 2–4 and weave. Treadle 1–3–5 and weave. Treadle 3 and make the first pick-up as made on treadle 1 for the first figure. Treadle 2 and make the opposite pick-up. Treadle 4 and weave. Treadle 2 and make the pick-up. Treadle 1 and make the opposite pick-up. Treadle 3–5 and weave. And so continue.

Of course other simple figures may be woven in the same manner— chevrons, diamonds and so on.

In weaving on the (a') tie-up, one of the plain-weave sheds must be taken up on the pick-up stick when making the pick-up on treadle 3. The other plain shed is woven on treadle 4. The plain bars on the sinking shed tie-up require the use of the pick-up stick also. For instance for the 1–2–5 shed, treadle 1 and insert the pick-up stick. Treadle 2–4 and weave. And so on. Simple enough but requiring concentration.

This weave is not advised for beginners.

III. A PERUVIAN THREE–COLOR WEAVE. The weave at (*b*) **Diagram No. 26** is a Peruvian three-color weave and is woven exactly like the Estonian at (*a*), **Diagram No. 25,** except that there are three colors, which make it necessary to make two pick-ups. And the wrong

Illustration No. 25

Peruvian three-color weaving. Left, draft (*b*) Diagram 26; right, draft (*c*) Diagram 26

side is not exactly like the right side. The plain bars are woven using treadles 1, 2, or 3 together with one or the other of the plain weave treadles, 6 or 7. To weave the upper figure as shown on the sketch, treadle 1–6 and weave, treadle 4 and weave. Treadle 1 and make the first pick-up, taking up four threads at the center of the figure. Treadle 3 and take up all the threads on either side of the dark pick-up. Treadle 7 and weave. Treadle 5 and weave.

For the next pick-up, treadle 1 and take up the threads of the dark edge. Treadle 3 and take up the threads on either side of the dark pick-up. Treadle 2 and take up the threads at the center between the two arms of the dark edge. Treadle 6 and weave. Treadle 4 and weave. And so continue.

IV. ANOTHER PERUVIAN WEAVE. The weave at (c) requires six harnesses, but is rather the simplest of the lot in the weaving. It does not weave the same on both sides. The background and plain weave part of the warp may be in a finer material than the pattern threads.

For weft, use material in the darkest color used in the warp to produce the little dots in the background, which are part of the effect.

To weave the figure sketched at (c) on the diagram, beginning at the line marked "X–X" proceed as follows: Treadle 1 and pick up a black thread on either side of the center thread. Treadle B and weave. For the second pick-up, treadle 2–5. Pick up three black threads over each point, including the thread picked up first and the red thread (or other colored thread) behind the first pick-up. Treadle A and weave. Treadle 4–5 and pick up nine black threads at the center, including the red threads behind the black pick-up but omitting the one to the right of the black pick-up. Treadle B and weave.

Continue in this manner till the seventh pick-up is reached. On this pick-up, after taking up three black threads and one red thread on either side of the figure, treadle 2 and take up the first two red threads of the flower figure, weaving always on A and B alternately.

It will have been noted that the black pick-ups are made always on 2–5 and 4–5 alternately. The red pick-ups, after this first one, are made on 1–6 and 3–6 alternately.

If preferred, instead of treadles 5 and 6, tie four treadles: 3–4–5 and 3–5–6 for the black pick-ups, and 3–4–6 and 4–5–6 for the red pick-ups.

Or these four treadles may be tied and treadles 1, 2, 3, 4, as shown on the draft, omitted. If this tie-up is made, where a single thread is to be picked up, as for the points of a figure, the other threads that come up with the shed may simply be omitted. Tie-up is always a matter of convenience and should be arranged to suit individual preference. The reason for the pick-ups in the opposite color behind the main color are to avoid long skips on the back of the fabric which would tend to make the fabric too loosely combined and would cause some threads to take up more than others during weaving.

These weaves, though somewhat intricate, are not too difficult or too slow of execution to be practical for the hand-weaver who is beyond the novice stage. However, when one remembers that they were originally produced on the primitive body loom and that they were devised and widely practiced by people we are apt to think of as "simple savages," one is led to wonder whether the average I. Q. of the human race is not perhaps much the same for the savage and the civilized man, and from prehistoric times to today. The so-called "texture weaving" of our times certainly appears childish and inept when compared with these subtle and beautiful things that were common practice in prehistoric times.

PART VII

—— *Four Guatemalan Belt-Weaves* ——

GUATEMALA, to the hand-weaver, is one of the most interesting countries in the world, for here all weaving is still hand-weaving and one may see beautiful textiles being produced on primitive looms like those in use in prehistoric times, and in traditional weaves and patterns that antedate the Spanish invasion and were probably ancient before Columbus made his great voyage.

It is true that the native arts of Guatemala are rapidly becoming debased by the buying habits of the usual tourist, but perhaps before all is lost some intelligent effort will be made to preserve the ancient beauty —as is happily being done in modern Peru.

Each little community in Guatemala has its traditional costume, different from all others. In many places the costumes of the men have been modified or completely replaced by shirts of cheap cotton imported fabrics and dungarees, but the women—always more conservative—still follow the old ways. Though the women's costumes differ from village to village in color and pattern, and also to some extent in form, they consist of three simple articles: a poncho-like blouse called a "huipile," a skirt which is a five-yard length of hand-woven cotton—usually dark blue, sometimes with white strips and sometimes with tie-dyed or "jaspé" figures—which is simply wrapped around the figure, and a girdle that holds skirt and huipile together.

The men also often wear colorful belts or sashes—usually augmented by a leather belt carrying a sheath and a long knife.

As belts and sashes are so prominent a feature of all the costumes, the weaving of these narrow fabrics is an important part of native life and has reached varied and interesting developments.

The everyday girdle worn by the women is usually made of a firm, stiff

97

fabric of the warp-faced rep variety, from three inches to three and a quarter inches wide and from two and a half yards to three yards long, finished as a rule with short fringes in a coarse braid. These girdles are taken several times around the waist, with the ends tucked in. The girdles for fiesta wear are usually much wider and may be decorated with any of the traditional pattern weaves of the district. These wide pieces appear to be heirlooms and are quite difficult to buy. The woman who finally sold me hers, after several hours of conversation, had to obtain the consent of her husband, her children and her old grandmother—whose mother, grandmother or great-grandmother for all I know may have been the weaver.

The fiesta girdles are different from place to place and conform to the traditional costume, but certain forms of the stiff everyday girdle are in fairly common use all over Guatemala.

Several of the Guatemalan belt-weaves have already been described —in Part II, dealing with weaving on the inkle loom. The simple tie-dyed or "jaspé" effect that is seen chiefly in men's belts and sashes, the striped rep weave—also worn by men—and the pick-up weave on the set-up shown on **Diagram No. 12**. These are all girdles of the everyday type and the weaves are not limited to any one community.

1: TOTÓNICAPÁN

The handsomest and most interesting of the stiff everyday girdles of fairly general use in Guatemala is the type made in the town of Totónica-pán. These pieces are interesting in color effects and are characterized by a profusion of sprightly little figures, most of them no doubt very ancient and often symbolic. The weave appears to be peculiar to this one spot, though somewhat similar girdles are produced at a place called Huehue-tenango, near the northern border of the country.

The fabric is in structure a warp-faced rep, like most of the belt-weaves, with a colored inlaid weft on the surface. When correctly woven, and well beaten-up as it should be, the fabric is very firm, with no long skips. No color shows on the "wrong" side and only a shadowy suggestion of pattern. For belts it is certainly an eminently practical as well as hand-some weave.

EQUIPMENT. In Guatemala, these girdles may be woven on the primitive type of belt loom, but are sometimes made on an odd little four-harness treadle loom that has no warp-beam and no cloth-beam and that somewhat resembles the little loom used by West African natives. The weave may be produced on the inkle loom after the manner of the Mexican technique illustrated on **Diagram No. 13.** However, as it is far simpler to weave it on a small four-harness or six-harness loom, threaded as shown on **Diagram No. 23,** this method is recommended.

The little Norwegian belt-shuttle with the knife edge, previously described, is the best type of shuttle for this weaving. In addition a small netting needle to carry the inlaid colored material is a convenience, and two small pick-up sticks are also required.

MATERIAL. Two different materials are used for warp in this weave— a fine white cotton for the foundation fabric and a coarser material in black for the pattern. As the pattern warp is closely interwoven with the ground, no slack results when both materials are warped together to the same beam.

In the best of the Guatemalan pieces, the black part of the warp is a fine very hard-twisted wool. This material is often difficult to come by among us and something else may be used. In the Guatemalan piece there are 110 ends to the inch over the pattern strip. The border is set with twice as many ends to the inch as the pattern strip. A coarse reed is best for a close-set warp. It merely spaces the warp, of course, and for a satisfactory beat it is necessary to beat against a flat shuttle left in the shed.

The weft material for this weave should be a cotton coarser than the fine part of the warp. For the setting described, a #5 perle cotton in white or a good grade of white carpet warp will be satisfactory.

A fourth material is required for the inlaid colored weft shots that give the weave its special character. For this, a coarse knitting worsted serves best, though in some of the modern pieces from Guatemala one finds silks or rayons. Cotton is undesirable.

WEAVING. A four-harness and a six-harness threading for the weave are given on **Diagram No. 27,** together with the corresponding tie-ups.

All the weaving is, oddly enough, done on the two plain-weave

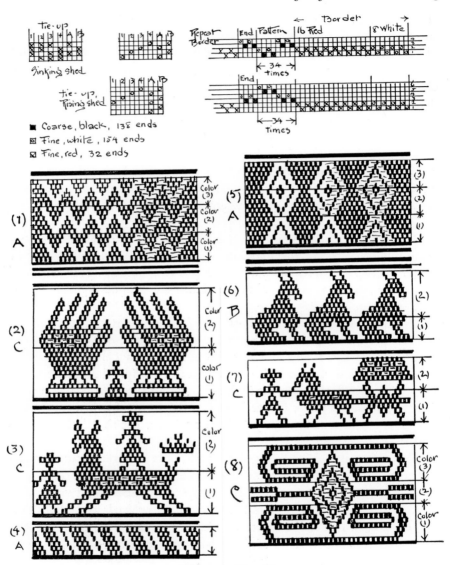

Diagram No. 27

sheds,—treadles A and B. Treadle A raises all the black threads, and treadle B all the white threads, and when these two treadles are woven alternately, an effect of cross-wise stripes in black and white is the result. This is similar to the South American set-up on the inkle loom. The ends of the piece are woven in this plain cross-barred effect, which is also introduced between the pattern figures.

The figures are woven in three ways which differ slightly and which I have indicated on the diagram as *A*, *B* and *C*. For *A* the figures are picked up in black only. For *B* the figures are picked up in black and the background spaces are picked up in white, while for *C* these two effects are combined.

The plain weaving should end on treadle A, which produces the black bar, and the first pick-up of the figure should follow.

In detail, to produce pattern (*1*) **Diagram No. 27,** treadle 1, which brings up half the black threads in pairs. If the four-harness threading has been used, the borders will also come up, but in making the pick-up, ignore the border threads, and beginning at the right, pick up four pairs of black threads on the pick-up stick; skip one pair, take up four pairs, skip one and so continue all across.

With the stick in place, weave *B* and then *A*, beating against the shuttle, left in the shed. With the fingers or a netting needle, take the colored inlay yarn under the raised threads of the pattern, across the pattern only, omitting the borders. Make the second pick-up on treadle 3, which raises the other half of the black warp. Take up four pairs, beginning at the right, skip two, pick up three and so all across. Weave *B* and *A* under the pick-up and insert the colored inlay.

This is the complete process. It will, I am sure, be found simple enough to follow the pattern as shown on the diagram.

In the *A* type of pattern, the inlaid colored weft covers the background in short skips between the black figures, as indicated on the right-hand side of the drawing and omitted the rest of the way for the sake of clearness. As these skips are never longer than over two black pairs, patterns of this type are limited to fairly small geometric figures, such as pattern (*4*) and pattern (*5*) shown on the diagram. Of course many other patterns of this kind are possible, and will suggest themselves to the weaver.

For figures of the *B* type, the procedure is similar, though the background as well as the pattern is picked up. Treadle 1 or 3 as the pattern demands—treadle 3 raises the first and last of the pairs of pattern threads, while treadle 1 raises the second and next-to-the-last pairs. It makes a difference in the count with which shed one begins. For instance pattern (*1*) began on treadle 1 as noted and pattern (*5*) as shown on the diagram begins on treadle 3.

Make the pick-up of pairs of black threads for the figure exactly as before, then if the pattern pick-up was on 1, treadle 2 and pick up pairs of white threads across the background. Use a second pick-up stick. If the second stick is taken under the black threads raised by the first stick, as well as under the white threads of the background, the first stick may be withdrawn. Weave *B* and *A*, and put in the colored inlay.

When the pattern pick-up is on treadle 3 the corresponding white pick-up is on treadle 4.

In patterns of the *B* type there are no skips of the colored inlay and the color effect is not as rich as in patterns of type *A*.

In patterns of the *C* type, the pattern and background are picked up as above, but occasional skips of the inlay are introduced by skipping a single black pair and not picking up a white pair in the resulting space. As, for instance, in pattern (*14.*)

The figures shown on **Diagrams 27–30** have been sketched from Guatemalan pieces. Many figures are used in each piece, some with slight variations. They are no doubt all traditional. One figure—that of the hands shown in (*2*) and the large single hand shown at (*15*)—are in all the Totónicapán pieces. I was told that this hand commemorates the last of the Quiché kings, who was killed by the Spaniards. Pattern (*33*) is undoubtedly the two-headed eagle which is a tribal symbol, far more ancient than the German double eagle. Pattern (*14*) is probably an armadillo; the butterfly in pattern (*16*), the cock in pattern (*17*) and the deer in pattern (*18*) are fairly recognizable. The lines of dancing figures in (*11*) and (*12*) probably represent a dance or "baile"—they always are woven one above the other in the typical pieces. Just what some of the other birds and beasts may be, who can say? At any rate they are lively and decorative. The pattern possibilities are practically limitless. I have selected for illustration only the figures that seemed to me most amusing. There is nothing to keep the weaver from "making his own."

A word about the colors used for the inlay. These should be clear,

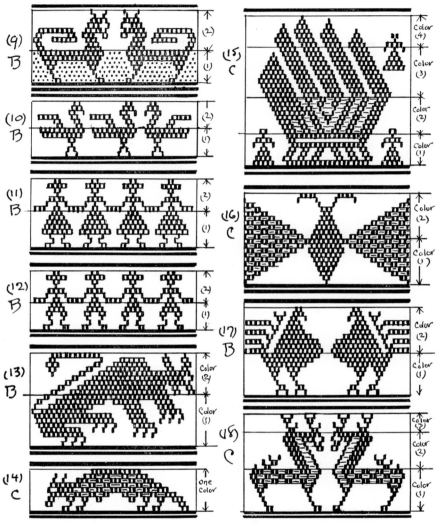

Diagram No. 28

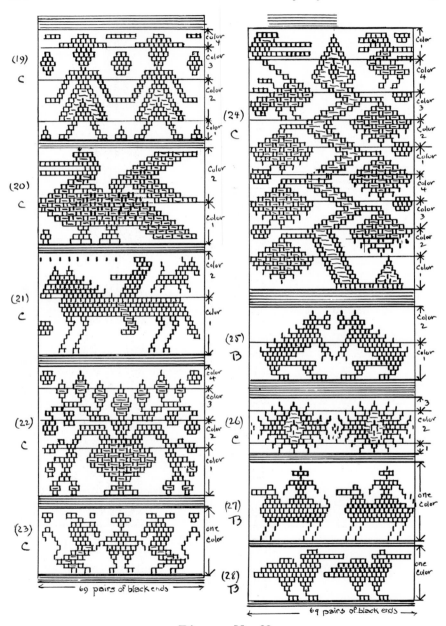

Diagram No. 29

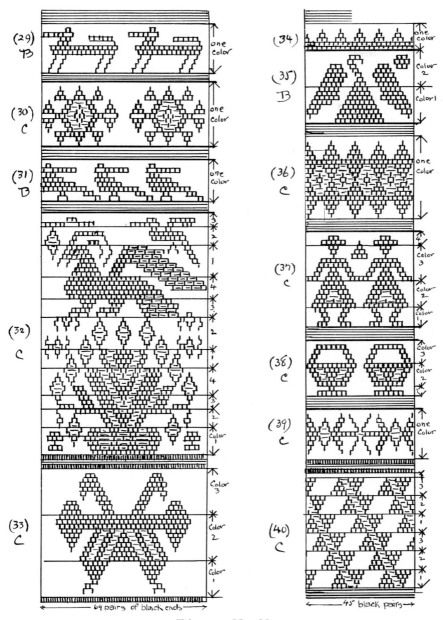

Diagram No. 30

brilliant shades, no very dark colors and no very light colors, but as many as one cares to use. Note in the piece in **Illustration No. 26,** that, though the bands of color are in various widths, an orderly succession of colors is maintained throughout. This imparts a pleasant rhythm to the whole effect though not apparent at first glance. These color rhythms are a subtlety of Guatemalan weaving, found in other weaves as well as in these belt fabrics.

Some of the narrow figures are woven with the same color throughout, but most of the figures show several changes of color. For instance in pattern (*40*), there is a change of color after each four pick-ups.

I find it good practice to measure off the length of yarn required for the inlay each time, for this prevents wastage and confusion.

In the girdles from Huehuetenango, which are far less popular in Guatemala than those from Totónicapán, only one or two figures are used in each piece and usually only one color in the inlay, which is taken under the pattern pick-up only. The effect, naturally, is far less exuberant.

Though in Guatemala only narrow pieces are woven in this style, on our looms we may weave as wide as we please. The fabric is handsome for purses, chair-seats, foot-stool covers and so on. It is a very solid fabric when firmly beaten up—as it should be. I have used it successfully for rugs done in coarse material.

As for most close-set warp-face fabrics, to get a good beat, it is necessary to use a flat shuttle—knife-edged if possible—left in the shed, to beat against.

2: A ONE–SKIP PATTERN

An interesting little one-skip weave for belts is shown on **Diagram No. 31.** I do not know in what place in Guatemala this weave is produced, but perhaps it does not matter greatly. I have seen only a few samples.

EQUIPMENT. This weave is most conveniently produced on a small harness loom, though it would be possible to make it on the inkle loom if one wished. It differs from most of the belt-weaves in that the pattern is in weft skips.

Illustration No. 26

Guatemalan girdle, from Totónicapán

107

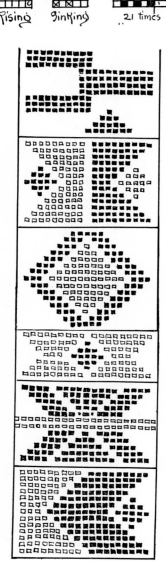

Diagram No. 31

The patterns used are usually quite simple geometric figures done in two colors, as illustrated on the diagram. Many similar figures will suggest themselves to the weaver.

MATERIALS. The warp for this weave should be a fine cotton set closer than for a 50–50 tabby fabric but not as close as for the Totónicapán belt-weave. This may be white or in a color. For the plain weave foundation fabric, a cotton weft, somewhat coarser than the warp, but in the same color, should be used. For the pattern, a quite heavy wool or strand cotton or silk or rayon material may be used.

The threading as given on **Diagram No. 31** gives an excellent effect but if a shorter skip is desired the threading may be: 1,2,1,3 and repeat, making a skip of three threads instead of five.

WEAVING. The body of the weaving is on the two plain-weave sheds, A and B treadles on the tie-ups as given on the diagram. The colored pattern material may be carried on small shuttles or may simply be inserted with the fingers. Simply treadle on 1 and put in the pattern weft, leaving the ends under the web. Weave the two plain sheds and repeat. Nothing could be simpler.

The results are surprisingly interesting, if many bright colors are used, and for quick and easy belt-making this technique can be recommended. However it is a weave for the bold in spirit. If done in very fine material and dull or light colors it would prove very disappointing.

The weave is suitable for wider fabrics on a large loom, and is excellent for such pieces as table mats, and so on. The weave is given in my "Shuttle-craft Bcok," revised edition, pages 311, 312, 313, where additional patterns suitable for belts may also be found.

As a rule, in belt-making in this weave, a space of an inch and a half to two inches in plain weave is introduced between the pattern figures.

3: AGUAS CALIENTES

An interesting and simple weave used for the stiff everyday belts worn by Guatemalan women is shown in **Diagram No. 32.**

The weave may be produced on the inkle loom if one likes—the method will be apparent—but may be woven more easily on a small four-harness loom, threaded as indicated.

I was unable to determine in just which community of Guatemala this weave originates, as it appeared to be of fairly wide distribution, but the pieces I procured were found in Aguas Calientes, so this may be the home of the technique.

MATERIAL. The warp should be in cotton, fairly fine—say a 24/3—in black and white, the warp set close enough to cover the weft completely. The foundation weft should be a white cotton, coarser than the warp. A good grade of carpet warp will serve. In addition there should be a much coarser colored material for the pattern effect. A number of colors may be used.

WEAVING. Treadle and weave as indicated in the diagram. If several colors are used, these should be woven in regular succession to produce the desirable color-rhythm as previously noted.

This is a very simple little weave and not spectacular in effect, though agreeable when done in good colors. It is a firm fabric and practical for other purposes as well as for belts and other narrow fabrics. On a large loom, it may be woven for upholstery, as it is a firm fabric without skips, and the fact that the wrong side is uninteresting is not important.

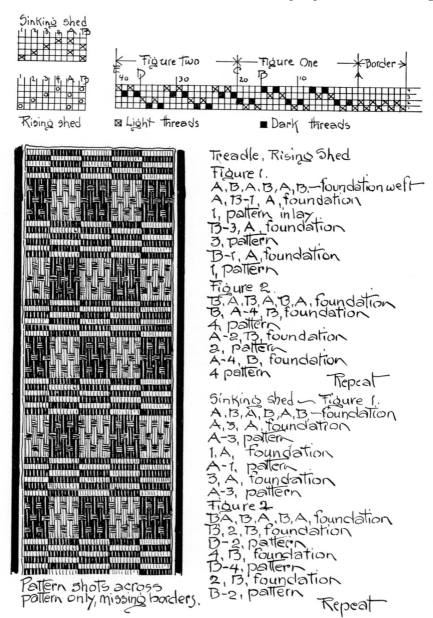

Sinking shed

Rising shed

⊠ Light threads   ■ Dark threads

Treadle, Rising Shed

Figure 1.
A, B, A, B, A, B, — foundation weft
A, B-1, A, foundation
1, pattern in lay
B-3, A, foundation
3, pattern
B-1, A, foundation
1, pattern

Figure 2.
B, A, B, A, B, A, foundation
B, A-4, B, foundation
4, pattern
A-2, B, foundation
2, pattern
A-4, B, foundation
4 pattern   Repeat

Sinking shed — Figure 1.
A, B, A, B, A, B — foundation
A, 3, A, foundation
A-3, pattern
1, A, foundation
A-1, pattern
3, A, foundation
A-3, pattern

Figure 2
BA, B, A, B, A, foundation
B, 2, B, foundation
B-2, pattern
4, B, foundation
B-4, pattern
2, B, foundation
B-2, pattern   Repeat

Pattern shots across
pattern only, missing borders.

Diagram No. 32

4: GUATEMALAN HEAD–BAND

An odd headdress is worn by the women in some districts of Guatemala. It consists of a long, stiff, narrow band that is wound 'round and 'round the head to form a sort of halo. No doubt it has a practical use in cushioning and steadying the baskets and bundles usually carried about on the head by the women of that country.

These pieces are done in a form of tapestry I have not seen elsewhere except among some Peruvian fabrics. Instead of the usual types of tapestry that require only two sheds, these pieces are woven on four sheds, and the weft lines do not always lie at right angles to the warp but may be woven in curves and slants to suit the design.

Though head-bands of this type would not be of practical use to our weavers, the technique might be adapted to the weaving of belts and girdles with interesting results.

Many different figures are used in these pieces among which the commonest are a recognizable rabbit, a swan, flying birds and geometric figures. Sometimes also humanesque figures, as shown on the head-band in the **Frontispiece.**

The piece illustrated is a "fiesta" head-band, woven of silk, and is five yards long, with elaborate end-fringes. It is worn with the tassels dangling over the ears. The everyday head-band is shorter and is worn with the ends tucked in, and is usually woven in cotton. Many different colors are used, though red usually predominates, as in most Guatemalan weaving.

EQUIPMENT. Tapestry as usually woven is a two-harness weave that produces the texture of a weft-faced rep. Tapestry bands of this sort may be woven on the inkle loom, as previously noted, but the odd weave of the head-bands requires four sheds and for our use a small four-harness loom is the most convenient equipment.

MATERIAL. The fiesta head-bands, as noted above, are often woven in silk, or they may be done in rayon, but the ordinary bands are of fine cotton, warped and woven in strands of several ends.

The warp of the piece sketched was of 36 strands—the edge strand

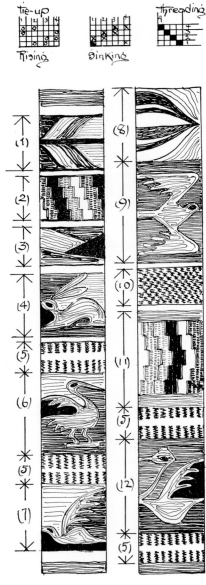

tie-up   threading

Rising   Sinking

Guatemalan · Head-Band

Diagram No. 33

on either side of 12 ends and the rest of four ends each, at a setting of 24 strands to the inch. A single coarse strand would not give the same effect. The warp was stiffened in some way, perhaps with starch. The weft was a two-thread strand, not starched, and beaten close to cover the warp completely. For the beating, the knife-edged shuttle, with the addition perhaps of a small comb, should be used. The reed serves merely to keep the warp in order.

The background for the figures—usually in several colors—is woven more or less straight across, but in the figures themselves, the weft follows the contour of the figure. And instead of plain weave the treadling is in twill order, treadles 1,2,3,4 being woven in that order throughout.

The figures shown on the sketch at (*1*), (*3*) and (*8*) may be highly stylized symbols of some kind, but the meaning appears to be lost. The rabbit is a tribal symbol and the birds are apparently purely decorative.

The figures are usually separated by spaces in plain color and set off by bands in conventional weaves as shown on the sketch at (*2*), (*5*), (*10*) and (*11*). The figures at (*2*) and (*11*) are woven in the manner of kilim, with open slits along the perpendicular lines; "opposite" treadles are used, as 1 against 3 or 2 against 4. A separate strand of colored weft is used for each three-strand unit of the weave.

The figures at (2) and (10) are woven on all four sheds: 1, dark; 2, dark; 3, light; 4, light, and repeat as desired to a middle stripe all in a light color or as at (10): 1, dark, 2, dark, 3, light; 4, light; 1,2,3,4 dark; 1, 2, light; 3,4, dark, and repeat.

The effect of this weave is lively and amusing and the figures are carried out with great freedom. This is, however, not a rapid form of weaving.

Illustration No. 27

African belt weave from the Atlas Mountains

114

PART VIII

Miscellaneous

UNDER this title I am combining three weaves that have nothing in common except that they do not require elaborate equipment, that they are handsome and useful, and unfamiliar to most hand weavers.

1: AN AFRICAN GIRDLE

This unusual weave I saw first in Vancouver, B. C., Canada. One of the weavers attending my class at the University of British Columbia wore a very handsome silk girdle she had purchased in London, England, at an exhibition of the handicrafts of many countries. She did not know where the piece originated. My guess was North Africa. As a class project we worked out the weave and set it up on one of the looms—in the colors of the original but in mercerized cotton instead of silk. The sample shown in **Illustration 27** was made at that time.

Later I saw an almost identical piece in the Art Museum at Montreal and was delighted to learn its native habitat. This was a district of the Atlas Mountains, where it was reserved for the adornment of the chiefs of a native tribe.

The effect is very showy, and though the weave is extremely simple it is produced in an odd manner.

EQUIPMENT. Just what type of loom is used in the Atlas Mountains I do not know. Perhaps the little treadle loom used by the natives of Sierra Leone. It is shaped like an artist's easel, with two little harnesses dangling from the peak, attached to two long treadles. The warp is stretched full length between two trees and the weaver sits to the right of the warp. As the weaving progresses, the loom is moved along the warp. This would not be practical for a wide piece, so only narrow strips are woven. For wide pieces, these narrow strips are sewed together, the design of each strip being so arranged that, when the strips are combined, a large figure appears. Most of these pieces—not illustrated—are done in hand-spun cotton—natural for the background fabric with the figures in a simple brocade in a coarser, more loosely twisted, colored cotton.

MATERIAL. For our girdle, shown in the illustration, which turned out almost an exact copy of the original in width and pattern effect—we used a #20 perle cotton in vivid green for the warp, at a setting of 36 ends to the inch. For the tabby foundation fabric, we used the same material for weft. For the pattern weft we used #10 perle cotton in dull red and golden yellow, with white, blue and black in the borders at the ends. **Diagram No. 34** gives the threading and tie-up—also the figure in detail and a sketch of the general arrangement.

WEAVING. The decorative part of the weaving consists of four sections. The stripes of solid color shown at (*b–4*) on the diagram are woven: Treadle 1, treadle 2—without a tabby, using alternating shots in red and yellow. For the figures at (*b–1*) and (*b–3*) five shuttles are required—one carrying green tabby weft and two each in red pattern weft and yellow pattern weft.

To begin the lens-shaped figure at (*b–3*)—which is used only on the ends of the piece as shown in the illustration—treadle 1 and take a shuttle carrying red pattern weft from right to left under the five groups of raised threads at the center, and under one thread more. With the same shed open, take the second shuttle carrying red weft from left to right under the same groups and under one more thread. Weave two tabby shots in green. Treadle 2 and take both shuttles carrying red weft —one from right to left and one from left to right—under the six raised groups of warp at the center, and one thread beyond. Weave two tabby shots in green. Continue in this manner, extending the figure at each side, till the edges of the piece are reached. Then change to the shuttles, carrying yellow weft and weave in the same manner, diminishing on each side, till the figure is complete.

African Girdle
— from the
Atlas Mountains

Tie-ups

Rising shed

Sinking shed

Threading

208 8

Green spun silk at 30 ends to the inch,
tabby, like the warp. Pattern: Dull red and
golden yellow silk, — doubled

End 23 times

(a)
Arrangement of motifs

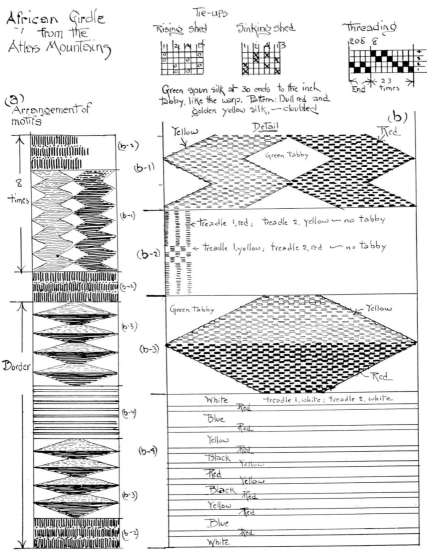

(b)

(b-1)

(b-2)

8 times

Detail

Yellow   Red

Green tabby

← treadle 1. red; treadle 2. yellow — no tabby

← treadle 1. yellow; treadle 2. red — no tabby

Green tabby   Yellow

Red

White   treadle 1. white; treadle 2. white

Red

Blue

Red

Yellow

Red

Black   Yellow

Red   Yellow

Black   Red

Yellow   Red

Blue

Red

White

Border

(b-2)
(b-1)
(b-1)
(b-2)
(b-2)
(b-3)
(b-3)
(b-4)
(b-4)
(b-3)
(b-2)

Diagram No. 34

For the original piece, this lens-shaped figure, in two groups of four each, separated by plain stripes of color, was woven at either end. The body of the piece was woven as in figure (*b–1*) repeated as sketched, the groups separated by bands as in figure (*b–2*).

This weave might be used to good advantage for table mats, or for draperies, or for borders in the gay little aprons that are the fashion of the moment. It may be woven as wide as desired and in different materials from those suggested, and as it is a simple technique, rapid and highly effective, it should prove useful.

2: SCANDINAVIAN WARP–FACED WEAVE

This weave, I have been told, is of Scandinavian origin, but I have been unable to find it in any of the excellent Swedish books in my library, and it appears to be unfamiliar to most weavers. As it is a handsome and simple weave, and does not require elaborate equipment, I am giving it here.

The pieces I have seen, made in this weave, have been narrow weavings, done in wool, and probably intended for use as ski-belts, though perhaps also for narrow, rather thick, neck-pieces.

EQUIPMENT.   As the weave is constructed on four sheds, a small four-harness loom would be the most convenient form of equipment, but the reed should be taken out and a small knife-edged shuttle used for beating as well as for weaving—in the manner of card-weaving and inkle weaving. The band is kept to the desired width by the tension of the weft.

The decorative effects depend entirely on changes in color, as in card-weaving, and many of the patterns for card-weaving might be used for this technique.

MATERIAL.   Medium weight wool and worsted yarns are, for most purposes, the best materials for this weave, though silks, rayons and cottons might be used. Very fine materials are unsuitable and very coarse materials make a very heavy fabric, with no practical use that I can think of.

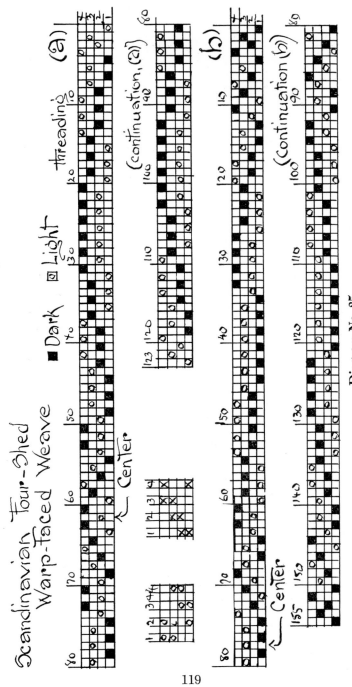

Scandinavian Four-Shed Warp-Faced Weave

Dark □ Light

threading (a)

(continuation, (a))

(b)

(Continuation (b))

Center

Center

Diagram No. 35

119

Two threadings are given on **Diagram No. 35,** and illustrate the manner in which drafts for this weave may be written. Only two colors are shown on the drafts—an alternation of dark and light. It is advisable to use the same dark color throughout, with the color variations in the light threads; or, if preferred, a single light color may be used with the dark part of the warp in several different colors. Of course several dark colors may be combined with several light colors if one wishes, but the use of a single color for either the light or the dark part of the warp gives a desirable unity to the effect.

The two faces of the fabric show similar patterns, with the dark and light color patterns appearing in reversed positions on either side of the fabric.

As the warp must be set very close to give the desired effect, it is best to omit use of the reed—especially if the warp is in wool—to avoid wear on the warp and difficulty in opening the sheds. It is not difficult to preserve an even width in weaving by drawing the weft to the desired tension. In the piece illustrated, the warp is a medium-weight knitting worsted; the pattern used was threading (*a*) on the diagram—a warp of 123 ends—and the woven width of the piece is three inches, or a setting of 40 ends to the inch.

The weft material should be coarser than the warp. A double end of the warp material will serve, or a strand cotton. If stiffness is desired, a coarse linen may be used.

WEAVING.   The treadling is very simple. In general it should follow the pattern, though many variations are possible. For pattern (*a*), treadle 1,2,3,4,1,4,3,2 and repeat. For pattern (*b*), treadle, 1,2,3,4 and repeat. Use a flat shuttle and use it after changing the shed as a batten to press back the weft. The Norwegian knife-edged shuttle is desirable for the purpose. As this is a warp-faced weave there is no take-up in the weft, which should not be woven loose but drawn to the correct width on each shot. As the take-up is all in the warp, a generous allowance should be made for this in making the warp.

This weave provides a very easy and rapid method of making handsome wide belts or girdles. But the choice and arrangement of the colors used is of first importance.

3: TWO EGYPTIAN WARP–FACED WEAVINGS

The two weaves shown on **Diagram No. 36** are very ancient Egyptian: (*a*) is a piece in the Victoria and Albert Museum in London, England, and (*b*) is part of the famous "Girdle of Rameses"—showing the "ankh" figure, now in the Liverpool Museum. The manner of weaving is similar.

EQUIPMENT. Just what type of loom was used for the production of these fabrics it seems impossible to say. The Egyptians used two types of loom as shown in various wall-paintings. They used a loom similar to that used in Greece, with the warp hanging perpendicularly from a bar, as in Maori and Chilcat weaving, but weighted on the ends with large stones. They also wove on warps pegged out flat on the ground, as I saw the Indians weaving in Bolivia. I cannot find any reference to the use of the primitive body loom in ancient Egypt—and this seems odd, as this type of loom was in almost world-wide use among primitive peoples from the beginning of time.

However, for our purposes, a harness loom is more practical.

MATERIAL. The material in both the ancient pieces is a fairly coarse linen, in the colors indicated. Other colors might, of course, be used. The warp must be set close enough to cover the weft completely when only one harness is raised, which means a very close setting and for a narrow piece such as a belt it is advisable to dispense with the reed and govern the width with the weft, using a knife-edged shuttle as beater.

The weft should be a good deal coarser than the warp, and should be in the color of the edge-threads in the warp.

WEAVING. Weaving is extremely simple and rapid. For (*a*)—on either tie-up—to produce the same figure on both sides of the piece, treadle and weave: 1,4,2,5,3,6,2,5 and repeat, or: 1,4,2,5,3,1,2,5 and repeat. If, as in a belt, it is unnecessary to have both sides alike, treadle and weave: 1,2,3,2 and repeat. If the weaving is to be done in this fashion it is, of course, unnecessary to make the 4,5 and 6 ties.

Pattern (*b*) is part of the border of the so-called "Girdle of Rameses"

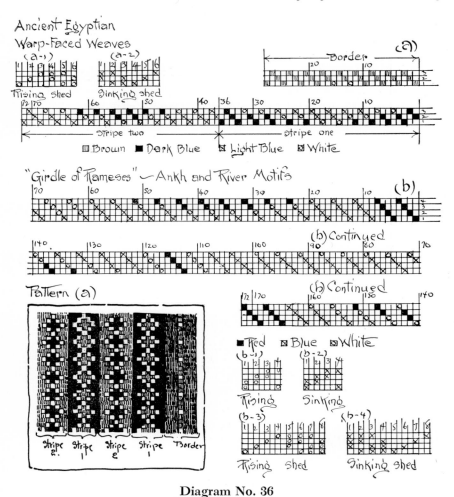

Diagram No. 36

about which there has been much controversy. The part of the pattern shown exhibits the "ankh" motif, which is an ancient symbol denoting life and prosperity. The zig-zag "river" motif indicates the Nile, meaning fertility and abundance.

The Girdle of Rameses consists of two wide borders in pattern with a central strip in plain white on which is rudely painted the cypher of Rameses. There seems to be no doubt that the piece dates back to the reign of Rameses, but some authorities insist it was a part of the trappings of the royal elephant and was not a part of the royal personal costume. Perhaps it does not greatly matter, in this day and to a craftsman.

The piece is finished at one end with an applied tape stitched to form loops. At the other end, the piece tapers to about half the width of the bound end and is finished with long braided fringes. The braid used was given in Part IV of this book.

It was believed at one time that the patterned borders were woven by the card-weaving or tablet-weaving method, but as the piece shows the same pattern on both sides and the warp-threads do not twist together, this is clearly not the case.

The colors indicated on **Diagram 36,** pattern (*b*) are the colors of the original.

As this weave produces a four-ply fabric, it is very strong in the warpwise direction and is quite thick and firm when properly beaten up. It makes an excellent belt whether woven in linen like the original or in cotton, silk, rayon or wool. The "ankh" figure may be readily produced in card-weaving as given at (*p*), in **Diagram No. 4.**

I suggest weaving on the (*b–1*) or (*b–2*) tie-up, though this does not give exactly the same pattern on both sides. It gives the same texture and is somewhat easier to weave than the double-pattern method on tie-ups (*b–3*) and (*b–4*). Done on tie-ups (*b–1*) or (*b–2*) treadle and weave: 1,2,3,4,1,4,3,2,1,4 and repeat.

To weave the same pattern on both sides of the fabric, use tie-up (*b–4*) or tie-up (*b–5*). Treadle and weave: 1,5,2,6,3,7,4,8,3,7,2,6 and repeat. Or: 1,8,2,7,3,6,4,5,3,6,2,7 and repeat. The latter is probably the method used by the weaver of the Girdle of Rameses, to judge by a recurring oddity in the texture that need not be described in detail.

We like to be modern and "up to the minute," but sometimes it is very pleasant to do again something that was "new" in times so long ago that they are now fabulous. So here is the girdle of the great Rameses —or his elephant's saddle-girth if you prefer—to be made again for today's occasions and adornment. This old weave has given me much pleasure and I pass it on in the hope that it will give enjoyment to others.

PART IX

Uses of Handicraft
—————— in Occupational Therapy ——————

It is hardly necessary to point out—at least not to anyone who is likely to scan these pages—that handicraft enriches living, by affording the satisfactions of creative work, the possession of handsome and useful articles of one's own production, the fundamental pleasures of skillful manipulation of the hands.

This being so, it is curious that the use of handicraft as a curative technique in sickness is a fairly recent development in the art and practice of medicine—not as new, to be sure, as penicillin and the other so-called "miracle drugs," but fairly new, nevertheless.

Experiments in "occupational therapy" were carried on in certain European hospitals and in a few American hospitals before the technique attained prominence with its introduction into American army hospitals toward the end of the first World War. The call went out at that time for people skilled in handicraft for this service and as one of those who enlisted at that time, I had the interesting experience of being a part of the early experimental work. At that time practices were not formulated and there was little or no specific training available. We "re-aides" of the period had in large part to find our own way. That we did a pretty good job, on the whole, seems to have been demonstrated by our results.

I like to tell about a charming Quaker lady who asked me to explain to her just what we were doing and why we were doing it. I did so to the best of my ability, and at the end of my little exposition she remarked: "Any woman who has raised a family knows that a sick child gets along better if given something interesting to do. But fancy those doctors down in Washington being smart enough to know it!"

The underlying idea of occupational therapy, however, goes a good deal deeper than recreation. Recreation may be all that is required in a short convalescence, but during a long illness or in the case of a temporary or permanent disability the patient sometimes drifts into a curious state of detachment from reality, and even when the actual illness is completely cured has lost his powers of adaptation to normal living. And this condition may be more difficult to cure than the original illness. It is to prevent this poisonous after-result of illness that occupational therapy is chiefly directed. Primarily, it is a technique in applied psychology.

Of course certain occupations may also be used to aid in the treatment of various orthopedic cases. For instance card-weaving is extremely valuable in developing "opposition of the thumb" which may have been lost or impaired, and to develop rotation of the lower arm. However the chief values are in the field of psychology.

It is not by chance that handicrafts are used more than any other type of occupation for the purpose. Psychologists tell us that our closest sensations of reality come through the sense of touch. We are all aware that things we see may not be actual, and that things we hear may be illusions, but we never for an instant doubt the reality of the things we touch. And as it is the chief aim of occupational therapy to keep the patient in the world of reality it follows that it is chiefly through the hands that the occupational therapist works.

As noted before in these pages, the small textile crafts described here are of special value in occupational therapy. They are—to most people—novel techniques and hence interesting, they do not make a demand on physical strength, they may be "graded" from simple enough for a child to intricate enough for a highly skilled craftsman, they are capable of producing useful and handsome articles that give the satisfaction of achievement.

Occupational therapy as a profession requires special abilities and special training, but an amateur home-therapist may find it very helpful at times to practice a bit of the art in the event of a sickness in the family, or for an invalid or a disabled member of the family who needs the help toward recovery or toward readjustment that occupation may give.

The following suggestions are intended to provide the amateur occupational therapist with a little help in meeting the problems that may arise.

It should be borne in mind that one may do harm instead of good—by giving a patient something so difficult that he cannot complete the project satisfactorily. This is discouraging. Or by providing something so simple that it is not interesting and so holds no pleasure. Or by giving a patient a project that excites him unduly, or one that strains his eyes or one that puts him into a strained position. The physician in charge of the case should always be consulted. A mistake may also be made in attempting to begin the occupational treatment too early.

In the acute stages of an illness or injury, and while the patient is in pain, he is pretty thoroughly occupied with his sensations, and the dream-state that occupational therapy is designed to prevent will not develop. After this stage has passed the patient is usually weak and is also occupied in enjoying the cessation of pain and the sensations of recovery. No occupational therapy is required at this point. But when the patient begins to be restless and irritable, in a hurry to get well and to be about his business again, that is the moment to introduce him to an interesting bit of handicraft.

Choice of a project is a matter of first importance, and the choice should not be left to the patient as a rule, though he may be given a choice among several suitable projects, if one wishes.

In the matter of an orthopedic case, the choice depends of course on the occupation best suited to exercise the desired part of the body—with due consideration for the psychological factors involved.

The chief considerations on the psychological level are two: the mental ability of the patient, and his state of mind—whether depressed and retarded or "disturbed."

The level of ability is important because to be a desirable project, the thing must be something the patient can finish, and finish acceptably. Failure is always discouraging, and not to finish something begun is also poor psychology. And of course to give a stimulating and exciting project to a patient already over-excited is undesirable, or to give a depressed patient something soothing and monotonous is almost worse.

To be interesting, the occupation chosen should usually be something entirely new to the patient, and among the small textile crafts presented here it should be quite simple to choose such a technique, as few—even among experienced weavers—have travelled all these byways. Card-weaving has proved particularly valuable for depressed patients, as much bright color may be used, the process is ingenious and amusing, and the work goes rapidly. This last is important because depression brings with it a retardation or slowing of all the reactions and a project that takes a normal person a good deal of time will prove endless for a retarded person. Moreover it is necessary to pay strict attention or difficulties arise. The thing cannot be done with the mind elsewhere. Projects in card-weaving may be made simple enough for a child of eight—though it is impractical below that mental level—and may be intricate enough to keep a high-grade adult actively occupied. On the orthopedic side it is useful —as noted above—in developing "opposition of the thumb" and rotation of the lower arm. It is definitely not a craft for a disturbed patient, who finishes too fast and too inaccurately and usually gets himself into very complicated messes.

For disturbed patients the most useful projects may be in braiding or knotting. The drawing tight of the knots seems to relieve tension, and the orderly and monotonous repetition of a set of simple movements has a soothing effect. Also it is possible to work at such a project spasmodically, dropping it and picking it up again at short intervals without too much confusion. The Maori twining is also useful for the same reasons, but plaiting is not. For some reason I have never been able to fathom, this craft is very difficult to some people—though almost childishly simple to others—and might give a great deal of trouble and disappointment.

To summarize: A project selected for occupational therapy should be (1) graded to the patient's mental and physical capacities; (2) novel enough to be interesting; (3) for a depressed patient, stimulating and not taking too long to finish; (4) for a disturbed patient, monotonous and soothing, made up of a repetition of a simple movement, requiring a fairly long time to complete. (5) The patient should be induced to complete a project once begun, and assisted—as may be required—to complete it in a satisfactory manner. (6) The physician should always be consulted—as to type of occupation, time the patient should be permitted to work, and so on.

Of the crafts presented in the foregoing Parts:

(I) Card-weaving: stimulating; useful for depressed cases; has certain values in orthopedic cases. May be graded.

(II) Inkle-weaving: stimulating, though less exciting than card-weaving. Plain weave projects are simple enough for a child of six and some of the techniques are difficult enough to interest anybody.

(III) Twined weaving: relaxing; a good craft for a disturbed patient. Not suitable below the eight-year level.

(IV) Braiding and knotting: one of the best crafts for disturbed patients. Permits wide grading, as between simple cords to wide girdles in the Peruvian or Osage braiding. For macramé belts in square-knotting and half-hitching, see the recommended books on the subject.

(V) Plaiting: a good craft for a disturbed patient, provided it is not found difficult. A small experimental piece is advised before setting up a project such as a scarf or a bag.

(VI) The weaves included under this heading are all fairly difficult— interesting and in the main stimulating. Should not be given to a child. Cannot be graded.

(VII) This group of weaves, like those under (VI), are not suitable for a child or for a disturbed patient. They are interesting and stimulating. Cannot be graded.

(VIII) The three weaves under this heading are simpler than the foregoing—within the capacity of a child of ten or twelve. Suitable for a mildly disturbed patient. Cannot be graded.

There are, of course, many crafts suitable for occupational therapy that are not detailed here: for children—the stringing of large beads, paper-folding, paper-cutting and pasting and so on; for their elders—knitting, tatting and crocheting, simple embroidery, the making of hooked rugs, basketry, etc., etc.

Some crafts as developed for permanently disabled persons, as for the blind, should be considered vocational rather than as occupational therapy—weaving on large treadle looms, for instance. Though occupational therapy may well serve as an introduction to vocational craft occupations.

And for most of us, a bit of personal occupational therapy is often indicated, in times of anxiety or periods of sorrow or distress. What can be more comforting than to turn for a time to something as old and as beautiful as weaving—something that has come down to us through the ages, unhindered by wars and famines, by floods or earthquakes, and forever new under our fingers.